W9-AOD-972

The Ultimate Digital Library

Where the New Information Players Meet

Andrew K. Pace

American Library Association
Chicago
2003

While extensive effort has gone into ensuring the reliability of information appearing in this book, the publisher makes no warranty, express or implied, on the accuracy or reliability of the information, and does not assume and hereby disclaims any liability to any person for any loss or damage caused by errors or omissions in this publication.

Design and composition by ALA Editions in Bembo and Optima using QuarkXPress 5.0 on a PC platform

Printed on 50-pound white offset, a pH-neutral stock, and bound in 10-point cover stock by McNaughton & Gunn

The paper used in this publication meets the minimum requirements of American National Standard for Information Sciences—Permanence of Paper for Printed Library Materials, ANSI Z39.48-1992. ∞

Library of Congress Cataloging-in-Publication Data

Pace, Andrew K.
The ultimate digital library : where the new information players meet / by Andrew K. Pace.
p.   cm.
Includes bibliographical references and index.
ISBN 0-8389-0844-6 (alk. paper)
1. Libraries—Automation. 2. Electronic information resources. 3. Online information services industry. 4. Libraries and electronic publishing. 5. Libraries—Marketing. 6. Digital libraries. I. Title.
Z678.9.P26 2003
025'.00285—dc21   2002015527

Printed in the United States of America

07   06   05   04   03   5   4   3   2   1

*To Sharon, Emma, and Eli,
without whose love and support none
of this would have been possible*

CONTENTS

FIGURES

ix

PREFACE

I have literally been writing this book in my head for five years, and I must admit to leaping at the chance to create it when ALA Editions first approached me. The topic—simply described as "libraries and vendors"—represents such an undercurrent to how I think about libraries and librarianship that the first outline spilled onto the page in a matter of minutes. Developing in four phases of my short professional life, my thoughts and opinions on the matter have shifted radically, even 180 degrees on occasion, but the central focus on the relationship between libraries and their private sector providers has remained solid. What was it that stuck in my craw? Why had I been thinking about this topic since the very beginning of my professional career as a librarian? Phase one began by accident, really.

PHASE ONE

As I frustratedly awaited word from numerous academic libraries about the prospect of entry-level employment (my approach could only have been described as "shotgun"), I did what many new library school graduates had done, and what many continue to do—I approached a vendor. The move seemed innocent enough. As it turns out, they were looking for librarians. They did not require three years' experience, a second master's degree, and at least one foreign language. But the real kicker? They offered me a job on the spot. Two simple meetings—an afternoon screening, and then breakfast with the vice president for operations—and I was hired, at a salary near the top of entry-level academic library postings that were currently available. I felt as though I had struck gold, that is, until I told the teachers and mentors who had spent the last two years teaching me the trade.

The looks I received were like those of parents whose children leave home to live in a foreign country, decline to take over the family business, or decide to marry outside their faith. Faculty, librarians, and library school colleagues expressed genuine concern over my decision. No one in library school had told me that there was a "dark side" to our profession. Perhaps the makeup of the student body and its teachers—mostly part-time adults and adjuncts, respectively, many of whom worked in the private sector—required that the topic be treated carefully. It never would have occurred to me that what I was doing could be equated with selling my soul, selling out, or worst of all, leaving the profession before I had even entered it. But since empathy and concern cannot put bread on one's table (the assistantship I had in the library was running out, and the offer to stay on at $5.25 per hour would hardly sustain me in Washington, D.C.), I decided to take a chance at a new job on a new coast in a new arena, web development.

I should note that some dissented from the majority notion that taking a job with a vendor meant exiling oneself from the fold. One individual, a businessman with a Ph.D. in library science, record management expertise, and a humorous and ironically open contempt for libraries and how they are run, said: "Good, you can do something that will make a difference." Another paid no attention to where or what I would be doing upon graduation. As someone whose opinion I cared most about, and after I had been faced with a choice between two departments at my new job, he gave me the sagest advice I received in library school, and I will always remember it: "It does not matter what you decide," he said, "it's your first job out of library school, it's going to stink no matter what it is." Not exactly a ringing endorsement, but seemingly better than the disappointment that others expressed at my decision.

PHASE TWO

My send-off complete, I left for the West Coast and the coming purgatory that one can only experience by working on a help desk, *any* help desk. But purgatory is probably too strong a word; boot camp might be better. On the phone and e-mail with literally hundreds of people from hundreds of libraries, supporting a brand new product (a web OPAC), it was trial by fire, sink or swim, do or die. Serendipity coupled me with the web OPAC (online public access catalog), and I will be forever grateful that it was not circulation, report-writing, or serials (not that those aren't really important, I was just glad to be supporting the public module). I learned more in two months, quite frankly, about what it meant to work with automation in a library than I had in two years of library school. I learned on the job, not only from the mentors and colleagues who had chosen the private sector as their professional calling, but also from the hundreds of librarians and information technology professionals who called, wrote, complained, and voiced praise about the products and services for which they depended on remote vendors.

Although vendors use the word "partnership" a little too loosely these days, there was a sincere sense of partnership in the relationships that were forged between this particular vendor and its customers. Moving up rather quickly to product management, I was able to take on a host of new web-based products and the clients who would influence their development. (My sole colleague in a unit that we were the start of came up with the title "product integration specialist" to encompass the post-development/pre-release specialty that we were convinced was needed; this unit was the seed for what would ultimately become a Product Management Department.) Admittedly, the focus is different from the vendor side, but the commitment, especially among librarians, and those who considered themselves such, was genuine. Believe me when I say that the people in the trenches at these companies see little of the riches that most librarians assume are amassed by everyone at a library automation company. The work is hard, the hours long, the commitment high, and the rewards modest.

PHASE THREE

Despite the modesty of the rewards, there were some payoffs. Foremost was knowing that the work that I did impacted hundreds of libraries. A common revolving door in libraries is that of an integrated library system or electronic resources coordinator to vendor, and vice versa. If the lure of managing a product for a company—and thus hundreds of customers—is pure, then the temptation to do so for just one library is more difficult to contemplate. Nevertheless, the lure of returning to the East Coast and an opportunity to work in an up-and-coming research library that did not use the products I supported were enough to make me shift gears.

I arrived at North Carolina State University (NCSU) pretty secure in my opinions, and secure in my abilities to make a difference at one library the way I had made a difference for several. What I did not know could have sunk a battleship. If working for a vendor was a technical and procedural boot camp, then life in a research library was an intellectual boot camp. Surrounded by an intelligent, motivated, and focused group of colleagues, my ideas and vision of the future of libraries would take new shape, change more rapidly, and be influenced almost daily. One thing, however, struck me—the way that many librarians viewed the vendors, publishers, and distributors to whom they were beholden. "If they could only understand how a research library operates . . . " was a common plea. Moreover, the vendor dark-side mentality that I had nearly forgotten about upon leaving library school had come back to haunt me.

Though I self-indulgently referred to my time in vendorland as "dog years" (not meant in a pejorative sense, but merely in recognition of the fact that I had worked long hours, with steep learning curves, for hundreds of libraries at once), I found that to many I was still "a vendor." I had never sold a product for the company (nor did I ever wish to), but this did not count for much. I was labeled. A common joke was that I had been sent as a plant, that I was a wolf in sheep's clothing bent on migrating the entire Triangle Research Libraries Network to the products of the vendor whence I came.

As I began to learn more about the operations, stresses, politics, and strategic planning of libraries, I saw the library-vendor relationship in a whole new light. I heard new frustrations, saw surprising fears, and was introduced to what I began calling the library-vendor paradox. The common complaint, as I've already mentioned, was that vendors, publishers, and web service providers simply did not grasp the needs of libraries. Since they were too focused on bottom lines and building new products that would sell rapidly, library vendors failed to recognize the expertise, experience, and know-how that libraries could bring to the table. I mentally paired this sentiment with the old feelings of disappointment expressed when a librarian went to work for a vendor, and rattled them around for a while. One cannot have it both ways, I concluded. Either the library world sends librarians out into the business world equipped to then deal with libraries, or libraries must adapt to endeavors in an uneven partnership. Under the current rules of engagement, libraries are faced with their ultimate paradox—championing the freedom of information in an economy and culture where hardly anything of value is free.

I was surprised, moreover, at how many librarians handled vendors with kid gloves. The relationship seemed more like dealing with an overly sensitive or reactive mate than with someone who traded products for dollars. (An interesting parallel can be drawn here in the way that some librarians approach a systems department; it is the technology, I contend, that sparks fear and trepidation, and not necessarily the people behind it.) I recall distinctly the shock (borderline horror, really) of a reference librarian when I decided to simply pick up the phone and call a vendor whose service, she had reported, was atrociously slow. "*People* work there," I said, "just like we work here." Vendors owe us service just as much as we owe them professional respect.

PHASE FOUR

At about the same time I came back to academia, something else was happening in the library world that would come to shape library discussions like no other topic since automation first intruded upon our field. The Internet, once that dangerous, uncontrolled, nonauthoritative, viral distributor of mis- and disinformation, was gaining in unbridled popularity. So much so, that even librarians who recognized it as an important tool also began viewing it as a threat: not a threat because the information out there was bad or dangerous, but a threat from companies on the Internet who saw the potential of the Web in an information economy, and saw it with huge dollar signs in their eyes. Business models would emerge that seemingly threatened the very existence of brick-and-mortar libraries. Electronic books were poised to replace robust print collections. In the wake of aggregated full text, both print journals and interlibrary lending services would drown with no one to save them. Artificial intelligence and search engine algorithms would suffice where humans once ruled. Real virtue, as the Librarian of Congress, James Billington, once remarked, seemed in danger of being supplanted by virtual reality.

Cassandra is still alive and well in libraryland: what was once the best and most promising career in a culture starved for information is now viewed by some as a dying profession. This is hardly the case. But before libraries either pack their bags for greener pastures, or conversely, dance on the graves of Internet businesses that wished to supplant them, they should take a long, hard look at the technology, business models, and service philosophies that these companies represent. Not only could these companies become our colleagues, they could represent (and in some cases, already do) our new partners.

US, THEM, AND WE

Libraries have built a fine house, but they do not own it outright. In the minds of some libraries, the landlord is at the front door, the taxman is at the back, and the wolves are howling outside the windows. It's time we invited everyone in for a sleepover. Strange bedfellows, indeed, but bedfellows, nevertheless.

ACKNOWLEDGMENTS

I t's easy to recall the things that friends and colleagues have done to shape my way of thinking. Sometimes the simplest turn of phrase or a conversation can have the most lasting impact. I would like to acknowledge the individuals and organizations that have helped shape my professional musings, without at all holding them responsible. My thanks go, in this chronological order, to Debbie Ozga, for getting me involved in that new medium known as the World Wide Web; to Paul Koda, who taught me (whether he knows it or not) never to take my profession or myself too seriously; to Ted Fons, who reminded me that I still took my job too seriously; to the North Carolina State University Libraries, which took a chance on a former vendor–librarian who had some pretty cocky notions about systems librarianship; to Michelle Rago, who taught me that web design is more fun than HTML code; to Mike Winkler, who helped me to think critically about academic librarianship; to Mary Ellen Spencer, who reminded me that I was not the only critical thinker in the room; to Kathy Dempsey and *Computers in Libraries,* for giving a fledgling writer his first international soapbox; to ALA Editions, for giving voice to a nonestablished, relative newcomer with serious iconoclastic leanings; and finally, to Karen Young, my editor, who, with astounding acumen, imposed a great deal of order upon some rather chaotic notions.

1 | STRANGE BEDFELLOWS

Libraries and Their Vendors

The beginning is always a good place to start, but the beginning of library relationships with vendors proves pretty hard to pinpoint. Nevertheless, this author is in the small camp of human observers who believes that humanity is destined—or doomed—to repeat history whether or not one decides to gain knowledge of it. With this perspective, history becomes an iterative pattern of stories through which humanity loops, doubles back, stalls, stumbles, and sprints, instead of a pile of compact lessons from which people learn through their mistakes.

There are two converging stories that make up the strange bedfellow scenario. The first involves a long history of libraries and the corporate concerns that built their buildings, supplied their desk drawers, and filled their shelves. This book, however, is not about buildings and book stamps, since the goal here is not quite so grand, in the first place, and not quite so boring, in the second. Nor are publishers a primary bedfellow in this book, because their history is longer and the focus narrower; though not a primary concern, publishers will be discussed insofar as it is often impossible to separate content from technology, or business practices from the ethics of librarianship. Library automation companies, online library service providers, and the Internet are at the heart of this discussion because of their singular (yet increasingly schizophrenic) characteristics, that is, technology, their short history, and their growing pervasiveness. History serves as the starting point.

1

BUILDING THE BED

Concerted efforts to automate library functions got off to a cautious start in the early 1960s, but had their roots in the efforts of a small handful of individuals as early as the late 1930s. The University of Texas was one of the very first to install a punch-card circulation system due to the tenacity of its then director, Donald Coney, and the persistence of the system's main proponent, Ralph Parker, arguably the founding father of systems librarianship. Parker even wrote a brief study for the American Library Association (ALA) in 1952, urging libraries to look seriously at the efficiency offered by IBM's Hollerith machine and Remington Rand's Powers machine.[1] Parker's first experiment with punched cards was with the installation of a circulation system at the University of Texas in 1936.[2] In subsequent published works, forward-thinking librarians mapped out the punched card's utility in ordering and acquisition, binding, cataloging, and circulation.[3]

It would be another twenty to thirty years before large university libraries saw the potential of internalizing the expertise of advanced computing. If machines were becoming so integral to the operations of the university and the library, then librarians needed expertise in creating, maintaining, and improving computer operations. With little or no operating expertise in this dawn of library computing, libraries were forced to rely on corporate partnerships, but it was not an uncomfortable relationship. Each side had its own area of expertise, and automation vendors viewed research universities as potential long-term customers for what was largely a lucrative computer hardware business. These partnerships—such as the University of Illinois at Chicago with General Electric, Bro-dart Industries with the Library of Congress, and IBM with *everyone*—would form the basis for the academic adoption of holistic approaches to library automation.

The mid- to late 1960s split libraries and universities into three camps: those who embraced the new technologies, those who took a wait-and-see attitude, and those who simply had no interest in them whatsoever. Schools at the cutting edge included Florida Atlantic University, the Massachusetts Institute of Technology, the University of Chicago, Washington State University, Stanford, the University of British Columbia, Harvard, and Yale. These last three stand apart because they essayed the first attempts to integrate mechanized routines into a single system, rather than concentrating on the implementation of separate modules based on departmental operations.

By 1968, librarians like Harvard's Richard De Gennaro were highly critical of the wait-and-see approach that most libraries embraced:

A major error in the wait-for-developments approach is the assumption that a time will come when the library automation situation will have shaken down and stabilized so that one can move into the field confidently. This probably will not happen for many years, if it happens at all, for with each development there is another more promising one just over the horizon. How long does one wait for the perfect system so that it can be "plugged in," and how does one recognize that system when one sees it?[4]

For 1968, De Gennaro's words seem prophetic, especially to anyone recently shopping for twenty-first-century library technology. But offering more than just an argument to allow automation into libraries, De Gennaro took early aim at a profession that was already trying to distinguish itself from its technically inclined partners. Keep in mind that De Gennaro was writing this more than thirty years ago:

> There is no reason why a team of librarians and computer experts should not be able to work effectively together to design and implement future library systems. As traditional library systems are replaced by machine systems, the specialized knowledge of them becomes superfluous, and it was this type of knowledge that used to distinguish the librarian from the computer expert.
>
> Just as there is a growing corps of librarians specializing in computer work, so there is a growing corps of computer people specializing in library work. It is with these two groups working together as a team that the hope for the future lies. The question of who is to do library automation—librarians or computer experts—is no longer meaningful; library automation will be done by persons who are knowledgeable about it and who are deeply committed to it as a specialty; whether they have approached it through a background in librarianship or technology will be of little consequence.[5]

Alas, De Gennaro's hope for a complete partnership centered within the library would not come to pass for any but the largest and most solvent university libraries. Despite valiant efforts by major universities to maintain internal operations of both hardware and software, the 1970s ushered in a new era of outsourcing and a recognition that most technical advances would occur outside of libraries, only to be marketed back to them later. The initial hope was noble, that hardware and software configurations could be shared among major universities, so that wheels would not be reinvented over and over again; but when the money ran out and the expertise headed for the private sector, libraries left to their own devices had to abandon homegrown solutions for more packaged (and polished) library automation alternatives. The collaborative spark would remain, however, and might even be reignited by new forays into library development of open source software, a topic to be discussed later in this chapter.

By the late 1970s, library automation companies began to emerge. Some of them came from the failed attempts on university campuses, some of them out of publishers' efforts to automate processes, and others as logical extensions of their existing library businesses. VTLS, Inc., is a good example of an integrated library system (ILS) vendor that grew out of its local beginnings at the Virginia Polytechnic Institute in Blacksburg to take on international significance as a creator of library management systems installed in over 900 libraries. The Library Corporation (TLC) had its roots in providing MARC-FICHE to libraries in the 1970s and 1980s, and grew into a major developer of library automation for public libraries. Innovative Interfaces, Inc., started with the "black box," which was the interface between OCLC and online systems, one of the first attempts at system integration for libraries.

By the early 1980s, the major vendors of integrated library systems had begun to carve out niches for themselves in the library market. Some of these companies went on to reap unprecedented profits from libraries willing to pay top dollar for the latest and greatest technologies available to their field. In the late 1990s, however, the Internet boom, and especially the pervasiveness of the World Wide Web, began to forever alter the environment of library automation, as new information vendors forged partnerships with libraries and with other automation and content providers. These vendor-to-vendor partnerships will have a tremendous but unpredictable impact on libraries, as it becomes less and less clear with each merger, acquisition, and partnership exactly whom a library is relying on for its services.

DRIVING DEVELOPMENT
Vendors at the Wheel

Despite what might still seem like divisive philosophies of libraries and vendors, there was, historically, always a sense of a common goal. ILS vendors and digital content providers served the desires of an information-hungry populace. Vendors with the singular focus of developing a product could deliver a more comprehensive and higher-quality product than libraries could produce themselves. This sense of working in concert caused only slight hesitations among libraries in building more and more partnerships with outside parties.

At the same time, the library itself was undergoing a bit of a philosophical revolution. Historically serving as gatekeepers of intellectual, cultural, and popular content, libraries began to transform themselves into gateways to information, more and more of which was not under their direct control. Most libraries seemed comfortable with this new role, since it allowed public service librarians to continue in their role as subject and discovery experts; it allowed collection managers to continue their selection based on careful criteria; and it allowed library administrators to greatly expand their collections and services without the traditional physical barriers associated with putting new books on shelves.

Until very recently, library automation vendors have driven most of the information technology (IT) development that is in use in libraries. For better or worse, the highest concentration of expertise remains in the private sector, and library vendors make daily decisions about which product lines they should pursue and which they should ignore. These decisions are not always in the best interest of the customer, and almost certainly fail to consistently meet the needs of the end-user. Even when ILS vendors chose to avoid developing products that had insufficient potential for profits, libraries were not the first to pick up the slack. Often, new library vendors would emerge to market these niche services and products.

At best, the current state of the relationship between libraries and vendors is highly productive; at worst, it is combative and competitive. An objective observer in the middle might call the relationship "strained." The catalyst of the current situation has been the advent of the World Wide Web. Ron Dunn describes the Web's information environment as one in which "the worst level of service a user will accept is the best level of service that user has ever seen."[6] Since the vast majority of online service and content development is taking place in the private sector, this Darwinian approach to web development leaves libraries in danger of being taken out of the loop of information delivery entirely. Moreover, it has driven library automation experts to carve out service niches that will provide the most profit and business solvency. How far libraries are willing to go along for this ride is yet to be seen; libraries that signify their willingness to work with each other and with their vendors to establish mutually beneficial outcomes will have the best chance to determine their own destinies.

Not all niche development has been driven directly by users. Libraries have had considerable success either in developing some of their own useful automated services or in working with vendors to make sure development progresses in a way beneficial to them. Niche development is interesting because it both explains the modular approach to the *dis*-integrated library systems that have resulted in so many library automation businesses, and serves as an occasional negative example of what can happen when libraries and integrated system vendors do not partner more creatively to establish effective development of existing products and services. On the other hand, niche products are perhaps one of the best developments to benefit libraries. Rather than build an integrated system that attempts to be all things to all users, some companies have sought the interoperability of smaller information sources and products that fit well within libraries' extremely heterogeneous digital environments. It is worth the time to take a closer look at some of these niche products and their development histories and inclusion in libraries.

"Full Text" Online

An exhaustive list of online content providers is beyond the scope of this study. Suffice to say that numerous firms have established themselves as serious content providers in the library and corporate markets. Like the printed indexing and abstracting services that preceded them (and that continue as online providers), the aggregation of content by parties only remotely interested in the mission of libraries is nothing new; there are, however, two important distinctions between the content providers of old and those of the Internet age.

First of all, the selection of content lies less and less in the hands of collection developers or even acquisitions departments. Online packages come as all-or-nothing collections, regardless of subject area, and usually make no price provisions for this shortcoming. Secondly, the distinction between content discovery and content delivery is blurred more and more by library vendors seeking vertical integration and one-stop shopping solutions for a demanding customer base. Libraries rationalize their inability to determine digital content packages by assuring users (and reassuring themselves) that it is the technology they are buying as well, or merely the online access to full text. Several ILS vendors are also taking this approach to marrying interface with full-text content. While this marriage might intrigue small libraries, larger libraries—especially the research community—should be wary of unmitigated content delivery. This trend, now known as "disintermediation," is addressed further in chapter 3.

Full-text providers are singled out as niche providers because they have endeavored so diligently to make their products stand out *and* stand alone. In this model, content is no longer king; in fact, distinguishing the exact content of some online databases is downright impossible. A heavy concentration on indexing, feature-rich interfaces, and personalized content delivery has shifted the focus from substance to form. The moving target of full text has even given rise to tangential niche services like those of Serials Solutions and TDNet, library service vendors who exist almost solely to list the titles and respective scope of coverage provided by full-text database vendors and publishers. These two companies are seeking to capitalize on the confusion created by libraries' own vendors. It literally took the effort of another vendor to make clear what should have been clear in the first place. While the solutions of these companies save several libraries from reinventing the wheel over and over again, the entire process seems a bit like throwing good money after bad. For reasons unknown to this author, libraries jump at third-party fixes rather than demanding the same fixes from those who did the breaking.

Interlibrary Loan and Document Delivery

Another niche, interlibrary loan (ILL), represents a prime example of integrated library system vendors attempting to be all things to all users. Self-assured that they could integrate the catalog—robust with record descriptions, search capabilities, and patron records—with the needs of library units with very distinct needs, ILS vendors quickly realized that they were in over their heads. Traditionally, many ILL units relied on paper processing and stand-alone procedures that set them apart not only from the rest of the library staff, but also from the online system itself.

It was only fitting, then, that stand-alone systems would present themselves as a solution to stand-alone operations. Library departments that had never known integration with the library's paper world proved less likely to seek integrated *automation* solutions. The integrated features that ILS vendors had to offer did not outweigh the features built into stand-alone systems that more closely mimicked the dis-integrated workflow of a specialized library unit. Couple all of this with a standards committee anxious to establish itself in library-to-library ILL transactions, and it becomes clear why ILS company development of ILL modules was doomed. At odds with standards-bearers from the early days, most ILS vendors embraced standards only with caution; fear often surrounded the development of products that might make reliance on one system over another obsolete. This is just one factor that caused the proprietary nature of integrated library systems to inspire a local development backlash, discussed further below.

Given these trends, the interlibrary loan market was ripe for stand-alone solutions like ILLiad and Clio, or even open-source modules like ILL Wizard or EDD (Electronic Document Delivery). ILL departments were anxious to embrace these solutions, since they more closely replicated workflows or intragrated (as opposed to integrated) internal office functions that were traditionally separate from the rest of the library anyway.

Course Reserves

Like ILL, library course reserves suffered technologically from its unintended segregation from the rest of the library. A perfect example of a library microcosm, most reserve rooms were left behind to perform nonintegrated cataloging, public access, and circulation activities. More akin to a small academic branch library than a specialized central unit, course reserves suffered in its treatment by ILS vendors for two reasons.

First, the integrated functionality of course reserves modules was, more often than not, an afterthought. This is as much the fault of libraries as it is of vendors. It could be argued that vendors moved to automate course reserve functionality about as eagerly as most reserve book rooms sought to automate themselves. In worst-case scenarios, libraries used the reserve book room as the libraries pasture—a unit in which to place librarians and staff with little desire to embrace technological change. Because of its microcosmic nature, very little retraining would be necessary; the reserve room was, in many instances, the last bastion of business as usual for libraries. Ironically, many reserve rooms are now overwhelmed by the technology that seems so focused on their unit—digital reserves, computer equipment and laptop circulation, and increasing interaction with technically savvy faculty.

Secondly, for academic settings with branches, some course reserve functionality sought integration where none existed before. Not only were reserve book rooms operated independently of the main library, but branches usually operated their course reserves with complete autonomy from both the main library and the main reserve book room. This made integration with the online system a losing proposition for both vendors and libraries; vendors do not want to deal with a single customer who wants four versions of the product, and branch libraries rarely want to sacrifice their autonomy for a lowest common denominator product.

Needless to say, the best opportunity for automating course reserves operations was presented to third-party library automation vendors. Without the constraints of ILS integration, more robust and heterogeneous products were developed. Eres, created by Docutek (and now used in over 200 college and university libraries), is just one such product that has come to dominate the course reserves market. The image-processing modules of these products also surpassed ILS development. Course reserves seemed a natural fit for the new demand on libraries to create, describe, and deliver digital content to the desktop. Most electronic course reserves endeavors would forge ahead while libraries, in general, grappled with the issues surrounding digital imaging and preservation.

Digital Libraries

One of the biggest areas for hardware and software development outside the traditional ILS, digital content management for libraries presents itself as the newest moving target in library automation. Sometimes as simple as scanning a document for electronic course reserves, or as complex as state-of-the-art digital management, access, and preservation, the digital library movement is probably the most perplexing and promising development for libraries since library automation began almost seven decades ago. Though this subject is worthy of its own textbook (ironically, the paper library on digital libraries is a growing one), the more humble aim of this work is to put digital libraries in the context of library-vendor and library–dot-com relationships.

With regard to this particular automation niche, it is easiest to justify traditional library vendors' reluctance to enter the fray. Nevertheless, advances in digital library development require that libraries pay close attention to the digital production arena whether or not any local activity is occurring. There are two important reasons for this. First, whether or not a library has decided to develop its own digital initiatives, it is more than likely that the library *subscribes* to digital content. Whether the content consists of electronic journals from JSTOR, electronic books from netLibrary, or digital images from the AP Photo Archive, libraries have a growing dependence on digital content that is not even remotely within their control. The demand for digital content predated, by several years, any establishment of best practices for the creation of such content. In today's library world, everyday decisions are based on the availability of this content, rather than on the quality or longevity of it. The same principles that apply to the acquisition and maintenance of traditional library resources should apply to the acquisition of digital resources. It's unlikely that libraries would purchase books produced on acidic paper, or a set of microfiche that did not include all the content that was purchased; it is equally unfortunate that the scrutiny afforded to these more traditional resources is not applied as readily to their digital counterparts.

Secondly, local digital libraries, in their infancy, tended to take off without paying much attention to best practices, standards, or the benefit of good business–model planning. (See chapter 4.) Moreover, even homegrown collections often rely on third-party applications for the creation of digital content. Libraries have been thrust into an entirely new arena of IT development, with a seemingly infinite array of hardware and software solutions available to meet the needs of any project. For libraries, certain companies have taken a front-runner position in the market. Luna Imaging, for example, offers a suite of digital services aimed at classroom delivery, file compression, and highly advanced quality imaging.

Another niche for libraries that got into the digitization game early is seen in the new explosion of companies offering data conversion services. Radical shifts in vendor attendance at conferences like Electronic Book (cosponsored by NIST and NISO) exemplify this trend. Early Electronic Book conferences (1998–99) saw vendors scramble to capture the device market for electronic books. Companies like RocketeBook and Softbook (now combined to form Nuvomedia, doing business as Gemstar, with devices marketed by RCA) fought for market share with web providers like DigitalOwl, netLibrary, Adobe, and Microsoft. In its latest conference (Electronic Book 2001, Washington, D.C.), hardware vendors were noticeably absent, replaced by software reader companies, several data conversion specialists, and an Open eBook standards committee desperate for organizational memberships and vendor acceptance.

A portion of the conversion services also involves the (relatively new discovery) of digital preservation needs. This is another area that confronts digital library initiatives, in that the needs of delivery must be balanced with the needs of longevity. Several libraries that had no long-term strategy for their locally created digital collections are now faced with major decisions concerning the long-term viability of those collections. The Digital Library Federation has made tremendous strides in the development of digital collection standards and best practices, and in compiling a list of resources and projects that member libraries have undertaken. More information on the organization, its findings, and initiatives is available from the federation's home page at http://www.diglib.org.

Electronic Resources

Of equally pressing concern is how libraries handle the description of and advertise ownership of their local and nonlocal array of electronically available resources. Most catalogers who have been around for a while will tell you that since the beginning of automated cataloging modules, one major consistency with the traditional card catalog has carried forward; this is the fact that cataloging modules are created to load multiple records into a system, and to create new records, but editing existing records has always been problematic. Despite two decades of advances in word processing, cataloging (and ILS development in general) has seemingly ignored the fact that anything ever changes with a data record once it is created.

This is one reason that the bibliographic 856 field—the field that stores hyperlinks to internal and external Internet resources associated with the title—first presented such a problem. The notion of editing thousands of records to include new MARC (machine-readable cataloging) fields was daunting at best. This author is convinced that philosophical stances alone could not make librarians resist cataloging Internet resources, but that the technological difficulties in doing so also played an important role. Vendor product development further supports this argument.

Despite their initial resistance to relying on the catalog to describe external resources, librarians quickly realized the futility of creating multitiered, hand-edited websites to describe these resources (in essence, cataloging the items multiple times in multiple places). As database-driven websites began to appear on the scene, some libraries struggled to create the ultimate "database of databases." The game was afoot, and the notion that libraries had already abandoned the real database of databases, the online catalog, is still lost on many in the profession. But due to the niche nature of the content, several small vendors—and some of the larger ones—would begin to develop various tools for managing description, display, and access to electronic resources, now available (ironically) with easily editable database front-ends, but having very little integration with existing library resources. Sometimes these efforts were even coupled with the latest advances in portal technology, adding a personalized view of digital resources, while (again, ironically) the only personalized access to an online catalog remained a carefully crafted subject-heading search.

The shame of this development path is the way in which many ILS vendors have chosen to catch up to these trends. Rather than upgrade the traditional modules of the online catalog system, many have chosen to pile on integration modules that allow libraries to link to the content that never should have left the catalog in the first place. Or worse, vendors develop entirely new modules that allow libraries to catalog, organize, and display electronic resources with absolutely no relation to the rest of the online database.

The success of modules like Clio, ILLiad, Docutek, and Luna is substantiated by ILS vendors seeking to integrate those technological solutions into their own products, and by libraries grappling with efforts to bring all of these heterogeneous solutions under the single umbrella of library ownership and patron discovery. A watchful eye on library vendor mergers and acquisitions should be kept by all libraries that have an increasing dependence on out-sourced technology and content.

MERGERS AND ACQUISITIONS
Vendor Conglomeration

If the early 1990s can be called a boom era of library automation, then the early twenty-first century might be described as a plateau. Once ripe ground for marketers, now there just aren't as many libraries around without some level of automation already. Minor attempts in the late 1990s to convince libraries that migration to other products and services could be made simple usually fell upon the deaf ears and buried heads of librarians who still viewed ILS and vendor conversions as an unnecessarily daunting and traumatic endeavor. Now strategies have shifted, as vendors who are unable to win customers seek to either buy them outright or to partner with other vendors in order to bring in a larger customer base. This trend, though moderately frightening to a profession that generally views monopolies as an anathema, will change the library vendor marketplace dramatically over the next decade. Though the outcomes are usually predictable based on similar historical situations, predicting the ultimate winners and losers is an enjoyable exercise in futility. It's worthwhile here to take a look at some of the most recent acquisitions, mergers, and partnerships. Grouped together, they present a remarkable trend.[7]

One of the most important acquisitions in recent library automation history occurred when Dynix and NOTIS combined to form Ameritech Library Services (later renamed epixtech). Many libraries had recently pinned their hopes on the new Dynix system as the latest state-of-the-art integrated library system. While still in its infancy, the company was acquired and morphed into Ameritech's new Horizon system, dashing the hopes for new academic library product development and strategy. (Names and features were swapped so fast that it is difficult to recall which system was for which type of user, but the end result was certainly dissatisfaction among academic libraries. Dynix continues to have a large installation base, but had no new name sales in 2001.) All three products, NOTIS, Dynix, and Horizon, came to rest under the umbrella of Ameritech, which itself would later change hands, its library automation division spinning off into the new company, epixtech. The tale is so long and twisted that, at any given moment, some libraries surely did not know which way was up.

The NOTIS/Dynix/Horizon trend would continue in the mid- to late 1990s. NOTIS Corporation would also go belly-up, joining Dynix under the Ameritech umbrella, as the marketing and development bulk of the company went on to form Endeavor Information Systems. Endeavor itself would betray its proud tradition of employee ownership when it became a wholly owned subsidiary of Dutch-based Reed Elsevier. To expand into the European market, Innovative Interfaces, which was privately owned by its two founders, would purchase, for cash, the SLS Corporation.

Again in 2001, Data Research Associates (DRA) was forced to abandon five years of development of its new product, Taos, when the company—which was publicly held—sold all of its stock to a major competitor, Sirsi Corporation. Late that year, the Taos product line was discontinued in favor of Sirsi's more mature Unicorn platform, and the Taos name already belongs to the ages. Other mergers and corporate changes also marked the turn of the century in library automation, the effects of which will likely not be felt for the next few years. In 2001, Innovative Interface's Jerry Kline bought out the outstanding shares of founding partner Steve Silberstein, giving him complete ownership of the company. Auto-Graphics acquired both the assets of Maxcess Library Systems and the WINGS Request Management System formerly offered by Pigasus Software (the latter deal is unraveling in the wake of a legal dispute as of this writing). British-based ALS International and Canadian-based Best-Seller merged to form BiblioMondo, Inc., in late 2000. The early twenty-first century of library automation is likely to be an era of conglomeration and merger that will give a progressively larger share of the market to the big companies, while smaller ones seek cooperative ventures in an effort to retain an ever-shrinking share.[8]

In examining the outcomes of this wave of library automation industry consolidation, it becomes clear that almost all of these mergers ended in favor of the employees and customers on the side of the acquiring company. More often than not, ILS mergers and acquisitions involve the termination of the product acquired and the expansion of the acquiring company's product lines. A rare exception to this in the early days of mergers was DRA, which showed unprecedented restraint in not only maintaining but continuing development of the two ILS products it acquired before being acquired itself; the Inlex and MultiLis systems remained viable systems even after Sirsi's subsequent buyout of DRA. Most other vendors—including Sirsi, in the case of Taos—made their intentions immediately clear to their newly expanded customer bases. For libraries, so-called synergistic opportunities meant the quick encouragement of product migration, or the daunting prospect of reentering the newly scaled-down vendor marketplace.

Mergers and acquisitions, however, might not always be to the advantage of customers on the right side of the product battle. The integration of business operations, phasing out of old products, and repurposing of newly acquired staff can mean stunted development efforts for existing product lines, while the new company maps its strategy. To others, it signals a change in focus of the company that a library thought it knew well. For example, Innovative Interfaces, once the darling of academic and law libraries, started marketing to public libraries, large consortia, and dozens of overseas customers. DRA left the comfort of the public library market for the financial gains available with academic libraries, and Sirsi shifted its development efforts from government and special libraries to larger and larger academic and public customers. This has the effect of pitting one customer against another, as libraries vie for the developmental attention that will take the library automation product in the direction that benefits them the most. As vendors try to be all things to all customers, they ultimately end up being less than their potential to anyone. In desperation, they even turn to each other.

VIRTUAL MERGERS
Vendor-to-Vendor Agreements

Like automation and computer solutions that drive other industries, the library industry vendors find themselves in a never-ending race to be first, or at least to stay ahead of the pack for as long as possible. Most have now realized that getting there alone is no longer a viable option. In the spirit of "if you can't build it, buy it," vendors are jumping (and betting) on the latest technologies that will improve their products. Sometimes this means simply buying the technology; other times, it means forming strategic alliances to deliver an integrated product. Either way, for libraries, it means entering into a business relationship with more than one partner when a single deal is made. Some of these deals have been highly publicized, and a few are worth mentioning.

INNOVATIVE INTERFACES

In the last three years, Innovative Interfaces has announced major codevelopment or third-party licensing deals with AltaVista (advanced keyword searching), netLibrary (electronic books), TLC (MuseGlobal metasearch), and Useful Utilities (EZproxy remote database access module).

SIRSI CORPORATION

Sirsi has also jumped on the content bandwagon, making deals with Syndetic Solutions and LibraryHQ (iBistro and iLink data streaming), netLibrary (electronic books), and Northern Light (Internet search engine).

ENDEAVOR

This firm's Voyager integrated system draws on a couple of major third-party offerings, primarily that of Microsoft Access, in order to generate various canned reports and lists. Endeavor also recently announced partnerships with Clio (interlibrary loan) and Syndetic Solutions (data streaming).

EX LIBRIS

Ex Libris has been one of the most active partners in the ILS industry, announcing major collaborations with Luna Imaging (digital asset management), Swets Blackwell (acquisitions), TLC (interlibrary loan), and Infotrieve (binding).

In some cases, companies that one would never have expected to work together now cooperate in ways that mutually benefit both companies' customers. This trend, which is as close as one can expect to get to vendor altruism, is noteworthy for its somewhat unprecedented nature. More importantly, the trend should encourage libraries to demand full disclosure of library vendors' business-to-business partnerships, since the success or failure of some of these endeavors will certainly affect the success or failure of libraries' implementation of these vendors' products.

THE "PARTNERSHIP"
Library and Vendor Codevelopment

Vendors like to describe their relationships with customers as "partnerships." In turn, librarians like to snicker at the analogy, given that one partner is paying the other partner a lot of money to deliver the tools necessary to perform the most basic job functions. Perhaps the term "partnership" is so popular because it avoids the slightly more accurate description—codependence. That is, vendors in the library market have difficulty marketing their wares to other disciplines (despite numerous attempts) and have traditionally relied on a rather captive, yet static, customer base. Libraries, for their part, are utterly dependent on vendors to supply the technology—and in several cases, the content—that make a library run.

From Codependence to Codevelopment

Despite the snickering and the semantics, it makes sense to think of libraries and vendors partnering together to provide a viable product or service, regardless of the uneven nature of the financial end of the partnership. Libraries do this to serve their own development needs; vendors do it if it means producing a product that other libraries might buy in turn. Moreover, libraries are more likely to buy new products knowing that another library has played a part in their development, as opposed to products coming out of a random marketing meeting or vendor strategy session.

Historically, it was usually local university computer science development that led to various automated systems, including those that ultimately became automated library systems. Today, libraries partner either formally—under the guise of contractual obligations or paid programming—or informally, through beta testing, local customization, or serendipitous codevelopment. Surprisingly, neither of these approaches usually comes close to the formal development process of either the library or the automation vendor with whom the library partners. Even more curious is the fact that this informal approach actually results in some highly developed and usable products.

Ex Libris (U.S.A.) is one example of a company with plans to take this development strategy to the next level. Traditionally, codevelopment between libraries and vendors has been an uneven playing field, with the vendor supplying most of the development and programming staff while also reaping most of the benefits, such as revenue stream, notoriety, and software maintenance fees. Libraries, on the other hand, simply receive a product built to their specifications; only on rare occasions does a library's willingness to beta test or act as an early adopter result in any real savings, discounts, or other tangible benefits. Realizing that this model might not produce the best codeveloped products available, Ex Libris announced that it would be offering premier partnership deals to libraries willing to supply various levels of expertise

in the product development process, including writing code, program specifications, and beta testing. Offers like this represent the latest in codevelopment opportunities and forward-thinking initiatives on the part of automation vendors. Sirsi Corporation has sponsored and encouraged research and
academic library symposia on various topics, and its Link Division plans further research library symposia on new product development for the company
and its larger customers. Ex Libris and Sirsi represent just two examples of this
sort of approach.

Communication and Collective Bargaining

When the relationships are less formal, communication is a key factor. In
some early research for this book, a survey was sent to twenty-nine major
library vendors, including ILS companies, content redistributors, and publishers. Question 4 from the survey relates directly to this chapter and is given
below. (A full copy of the survey is reproduced in appendix B at the end of
this book.)

> (4) Does your company have a forum for users (both individual and institu-
> tional) to submit feedback about your online products? If so, what is it? Do
> users take advantage of feedback opportunities? How is user feedback incor-
> porated into your product development?

Before getting into the details of the responses, it should be noted that
only nine of the twenty-nine vendors responded to the survey, putting a bit
of a dent in the argument that libraries and vendors have a common goal of
cooperation. The survey was sent as hard copy and was made available online.
An e-mail message was sent ten days after the initial call for participation, and
then again eight months later. Most respondents answered the survey completely. Others who asked for more details or promised to respond never did.
One vendor, Ex Libris (U.S.A.), actually responded to the survey both times
that it was sent; the responses were even sent by the president of the company
himself. The survey was sent to the following vendors:

Academic Press	Cambridge Scientific Abstracts
Accessible Archives	CARL Systems
Annual Reviews	EBSCO Information Services
Bell & Howell Information and Learning	Endeavor Information Systems
	Emerald MCB University Press

epixtech

Ex Libris

Gale Group

H. W. Wilson

Highwire Press

Infonautics Electronic Library

Ingenta

Innovative Interfaces

JSTOR

Kluwer Journals Online

Lexis-Nexis

OCLC FirstSearch

Ovid Technologies

Oxford Journals Online

Project Muse

RoweCom Information Quest

ScienceDirect Elsevier Science
  Journals

Sirsi Corporation

Swets Blackwell

VTLS

Those who responded to the survey were CARL Systems, EBSCO Information Services, Ex Libris (U.S.A.), Innovative Interfaces, Kluwer Journals Online, OCLC FirstSearch, Ovid Technologies, RoweCom Information Quest, and Sirsi Corporation.

Most of the survey respondents mentioned having some sort of user feed-back mechanism. These include, but are not limited to:

Users group website and discussion lists	4
Web-enabled comment submission	4
Users group meetings	3
Formal software-improvement request procedure	2
Customer-only website	1
Product management e-mail	1
Advisory committees	1
Focus groups	1
Beta testing	1
Library director retreats	1

Surprisingly, only one company admitted that much of its product development feedback came from its own sales force. Most libraries are familiar with this particular development strategy, since development obligations negotiated during systems' sales either move the product ahead quickly, or tend to bog down development that existing customers are waiting for. In response to the question about whether or not users of the vendor's service took advantage of feedback opportunities, five vendors answer "a lot," while three answered "occasionally" (the three options were "a lot," "occasionally," and "almost never").

Given all the organizing that libraries tend to do around certain interest groups, it's surprising that approaching vendors collectively is not a strong suit. For instance, quite a lot of bibliographic instruction effort is applied to various vendor interfaces for online resources. These instruction strategies are even shared cooperatively among libraries, and are developed collaboratively. These groups rarely get together, however, to approach a vendor with a much-needed feature, improvement, or bug fix. The closest thing to this model is the software improvement procedure adopted by major ILS vendors. Some of these processes merely placate customers with a sense that they are contributing to the product wish list that informs corporate development strategy; others go so far as to promise development on the most requested improvements. Certainly, approaching vendors en masse has more impact than individual feedback forms and e-mails. This collective bargaining approach might even result in some real improvement of service, such as standardized statistical measures from online content providers; OpenURL (a nearly standard way to format a URL with direct access to full text) implementation by electronic journals aggregators; or universal adoption and codevelopment of NISO circulation standards by the vendor community.

Libraries and vendors might also begin to reexplore sharing more in their relationships with each other. This can benefit both parties if done carefully and pragmatically. For several years, the Library and Information Technology Association (LITA), a subdivision of the ALA, had a vendor-library users' group. Interests split down the middle by culture and strategic goals found they had more in common than they thought. The group started off well, but interest waned among vendors who saw the meetings as an opportunity for customers to complain and competitors to steal, and among libraries who felt that vendors simply ignored cooperative opportunities in favor of product pitches and market hype. But there are new opportunities for collaboration that might not even require revealing corporate secrets or enduring product endorsements.

As libraries integrate disparate digital services in their own libraries, they often engage in a desperate search for an alternative that a library vendor has failed to provide. One solution might be to share product enhancement specifications with a variety of vendors, including ones not used by the library. This could result in the feature being made available to the library, and could potentially keep the price down if other vendors offer similar solutions of their own based on the same library needs.

In a way, the open source software movement (see the next section in this chapter) is a subtle move in this direction. "Free" software developers must contend with the openness of this development model that allows corporations to acquire, modify, and resell the software that was intended to be shared for free. A more direct approach—that of suggesting to the vendor that it might want to look into the open source software—harnesses the programming resources of that particular vendor, and leaves the library no more beholden to that vendor than it was at the start. This method is untried, but intriguing.

Vendor and library participation in standards organizations is another example of this approach. As the proprietary nature that sustained many library vendors for years begins to wane in favor of the assurance of interoperability, librarians and vendors will sit at the table together to work out the details of standards (and potential standards) such as Z39.50, OpenURL, Open Archives, and the NCIP circulation protocol.

Likewise, vendors should seek strategies that allow them to openly discuss corporate strategy, product development plans, and company direction. Their customers, in turn, can plan product integration, service models, and begin long-range planning in relation to the developments of their many vendors. For instance, a library may include a vendor's plan to incorporate multimedia into its course reserves software as a possible delivery tool for other digitization projects. In some instances, feedback to the vendor might even derail certain development plans in favor of others. For example, a library network of disparate library systems may urge its vendor to abandon plans for enhancing a union catalog product in favor of advancing the NCIP protocol for sharing circulation data between different systems in the same way that Z39.50 shares bibliographic data.

As these relationships are built and sustained, mutual respect and deference to contrasting skills will benefit both sides. As choosing between vendors and Internet content providers becomes more like choosing between two equally priced, equally performing automobiles, libraries may even see a day when library vendors begin to share their knowledge with each other. However unbalanced the relationships remain, the efforts at formal partnerships remain laudable. Other libraries, however, continue to consider their vendor relationships as mere conveniences at best, or as hostage situations at worst. Rather than integrate solutions with existing vendor-supplied products and services, some libraries have ventured out on their own to create their own automation products.

HOMEGROWN BACKLASH

This book is hardly the first to report that libraries have a growing dependence on outside automation resources. As a result, the niches and undeveloped services that were once only exploited by new or existing library vendors—or large research libraries—are now taken up by libraries themselves. Some of these projects ultimately wind up as major partnerships with vendors, but others maintain their homegrown nature, often by embracing open source software. Maybe it's history repeating itself. Maybe the lines between library and information science, information systems, and computer science are becoming so blurred as to be indistinguishable. Libraries, especially academic ones, are embracing computing and programming efforts in a way unprecedented since the era of homegrown library systems. More likely, it's the library profession's embrace of openness, sharing, and a nonprofit spirit that drives it toward local development and control. How this will play out for libraries this time around remains to be seen.

Open Source Software

The resurgence of homegrown systems might be a backlash, but it might be seen as coming full circle as well. Having once been the creators of their own automated solutions, many libraries are back in the software development business. From an industry that has historically made the best use of open standards comes a major foray into open source software (OSS) development, where library programmers and amateur product creators are churning out some of the most popular and fastest-spreading library software packages available. Put simply, OSS guarantees free access to the programming, or source code, behind a program's pre-compiled binary. This allows users to install the software and modify it, if so desired, to meet particular needs. It also allows for collective development among a community of software code writers. Perhaps the best illustration of this is the development of the Linux operating system, which currently enjoys widespread adoption inside and outside of the OSS community.

Most open source software is released under the GNU General Public License. The open source movement emphasizes freedom of use and distribution more than freeness of cost, as the basic principles of an open source license show:

- The license shall not restrict any party from selling or giving away the software as a component of an aggregate software distribution containing programs from several different sources.
- The program must include source code and must allow distribution in source code as well as compiled form.
- The license must allow modifications and derived works must allow them to be distributed under the same terms as the license for the original software.
- The license may restrict source code from being distributed in modified form only if the license allows the distribution of patch files with the source code for the purpose of modifying the program at build time.
- The license must not discriminate against any person or group of persons.
- The license must not restrict anyone from making use of the program in a specific field or endeavor.
- The rights attached to the program must apply to all to whom the program is redistributed without the need for execution of an additional license for those parties.
- The license must not be specific to a product.
- The license must not contaminate other software by placing restrictions on any software distributed along with the licensed software.[9]

In-house development, however, is not without its pitfalls. Libraries trying to build their own tools must determine if there is an ample return on the investment required by locally developing and maintaining mission-critical software services. The use of an open source product like Apache (web server software), for example, might adequately serve the library's web server needs; Apache has existed for a long time, and has a large base of support. By contrast, locally developed software code for something like searching a database or indexing important resources might pose problems if the software is supported by only a single programmer, or if it has limited financial or personnel support.

Like a grassroots movement run rampant, some level of open source development or use can be found in almost every library with an information technology staff or a web developer. Here are some of the most recognizable and popular offerings, in terms of their particular focus on library operations. Some libraries might not even realize that the software they are using originated as open source.

James, a Java API for MARC records

XML MARC, a MARC-to-XML conversion utility

MyLibrary@NCState, a portal for library resources

ZETA Perl, a Z39.50 module written in Perl

PHP, web middleware for web database presentation

YAZ, a Z39.50 toolkit

SiteSearch, a metasearch engine for multiple database searching

It's too hard to determine now whether the open source movement represents a viable backlash, or whether libraries are doomed to repeat a history that gave birth to many names on the present slate of automation vendors. Some projects—Serials Solutions is a good example—have already made the jump from being a locally conceived automation solution to a popular commercial online service. One thing is certain, however, and that is that the full development of a usable and sharable open-source integrated library system remains highly unlikely. Aside from being a solution for small collections with limited sophistication, open source as a wide-range solution is noble, but not viable. This places libraries, which will remain dependent on their current integrated library systems, in a difficult development position. Libraries are faced with a choice between codeveloping integrated solutions with corporations who have little interest in extensibility and platform independence, and taking a more open, flexible, and free approach that might never use to full advantage the proprietary software that runs the core business of the library.

In the search for a viable compromise, libraries must rely on two underlying trends that have affected both library automation vendors and libraries. The first trend is an ongoing reliance on industry standards, the use of which better ensures interoperability between libraries *and* between vendors. The second trend involves a more open approach to system development that has been embraced by one library automation vendor after another. No longer wedded to proprietary database structures, private tools, and closed source code, many vendors are meeting the open architecture demands of sophisticated customers. This openness means easier development of local services and customization of proprietary software. Paradoxically, it also means easier migration from one vendor's system to another. On the other hand, vendors are slowly realizing that making it easier to understand their systems can actually stimulate loyalty among their customers. That feeling of loyalty is something that the library automation sector's counterparts, online content vendors and publishers, can only dream of.

Scholarly Initiatives vs. High Profit

A scholarly extension of the open source movement can be seen in the initiatives formed to counter the rising prices of academic serial subscriptions. University presses have traditionally printed scholarly works that might not otherwise have found an affordable publisher, and have offered quality books at affordable prices to the libraries of the university community from whence they came. Would that it were so for scholarly journal materials. For decades, academic libraries have found themselves in a catch-22 of collection development when it comes to acquiring scholarly journals. Contributing members of academia, who are dependent on the publishing cycle for tenure and promotion, assign copyrights of their scholarly endeavors to large publishing houses, who, in turn, sell the content back to college and university libraries at tremendous markups. The inflation rates for scholarly journals are well documented within the library literature and do not need repeating here; suffice it to say that large publishers—and, ironically, even some scholarly organizations—have academic libraries over the proverbial barrel when it comes to building their journal collections.

The situation can only be described as dire. While the body of published scholarly work has doubled since 1986, the average number of the North American research library's journal subscriptions has actually declined by 6.5 percent.[10] And scholarly communication is big business. Currently, 121 North American members of the Association of Research Libraries (ARL) spend a total of $480 million annually on journal subscriptions; by 2015, it is estimated that this expenditure will reach $1.9 billion. The profit margins of publishers for this scholarly material run to 40 percent and higher.[11]

Scholars are losing control of a system that should be theirs alone, and it is not beyond them, or the libraries who bear the financial burden in this catch-22, to make a concerted effort to cut out the middleman. In response, scholars and librarians formed the Scholarly Publishing and Academic Resources Coalition (SPARC), an initiative of the ARL, as a counter to powerful academic publishing interests. SPARC serves as an incubation mechanism for scholars to publish their own print and online alternatives to the aggregated scholarship of major publishers. This peer-reviewed and peer-to-peer alternative has proven quite successful; as of 2001, SPARC boasted approximately 200 member institutions in North America, Europe, Asia, and Australia, and more than 20 successful journal titles. In 2001 SPARC announced the availability of *Gaining Independence: A Manual for Planning the Launch of a Nonprofit Electronic Publishing Venture,* a detailed handbook to help universities, libraries, and others conceive, plan, and implement alternatives to commercially published scholarly and scientific information. This new publication complements SPARC's *Declaring Independence: A Guide to Creating Community-Controlled Science Journals,* which SPARC and the Triangle Research Libraries Network introduced in 2001.

SPARC has also been helped by an equally successful marketing strategy, encapsulated by CreateChange.org. This cooperative effort, sponsored by the ARL, the Association of College and Research Libraries (ACRL), and SPARC, with the support of the Gladys Krieble Delmas Foundation, promotes the exchange of information, discussion, and action, and serves as an advocacy arm for its sponsoring organizations.

The beginning of this chapter warned that publishers would not be a main focus of the book, but it is increasingly difficult to separate technology and content in the world of library automation and resources. SPARC bears mentioning not only for the important initiatives that it has taken, but also for the model of business practice that it demonstrates to libraries. SPARC journals are not free in cost, but they are free of the grasp of corporate publishers who care more about profit than about access to scholarly research by the academic community that depends on it. Libraries can indeed beat some corporate interests at their own game. While one can only describe the new relationship as adversarial, libraries will benefit as corporate publishers mend their ways to woo back the audience that they are losing. The lessons to be learned from dot-com corporations are also compelling and much less adversarial, as the next chapter describes.

Notes

1. Ralph H. Parker, *Library Applications of Punched Cards: A Description of Mechanical Systems* (Chicago: American Library Association, 1952).
2. Ralph H. Parker, "The Punched Card Method in Circulation Work," *Library Journal* 61 (Dec. 1, 1936): 903–5.
3. Parker, "Punched Card Method," 903–5; Parker, *Library Applications of Punched Cards;* Robert S. Casey et al., eds., *Punched Cards: The Applications to Science and Industry,* 2nd ed. (New York: Reinhold, 1958); Paul Wasserman, *The Librarian and the Machine: Observations of the Application of Machines in Administration of College and University Libraries* (Detroit: Gale Research, 1965); N. S. M. Cox, J. D. Dews, and J. L. Dolby, *The Computer and the Library: The Role of the Computer in the Organization and Handling of Information in Libraries* (Newcastle

upon Tyne, Eng.: University Library Publications, 1966); Richard De Gennaro, "The Development and Administration of Automated Systems in Academic Libraries," *Journal of Library Automation* 1, no. 1 (1968): 75–91.

4. De Gennaro, "Development and Administration of Automated Systems," 77.

5. Ibid., 80.

6. Ron Dunn, "Internet Librarian Breakfast Session" (presentation given at the Internet Librarian Conference, Monterey, Calif., 1998).

7. This summary of recent corporate histories is based on various issues of *Library Journal, Computers in Libraries,* and *American Libraries* from 1996 to 2002.

8. Marshall Breeding, "The Open Source ILS: Still Only a Distant Possibility," *Information Technology and Libraries* 21, no. 1 (2002): 16–18.

9. David Bretthauer, "Open Source Software: A History," *Information Technology and Libraries* 21, no. 1 (2002): 9.

10. CreateChange.org, at http://www.createchange.org/librarians/faq/scomm. html#q1.

11. CreateChange.org, at http://www.createchange.org/librarians/issues/quick. html.

2 | SIZING UP THE DOT-COM COMPETITION

R ecall the service challenge posed by the World Wide Web in the last chapter: "The worst level of service that a user will accept is the best level of service that he has ever seen." So said Thomson Learning's Ron Dunn at the Internet Librarian in 1998. It's a maxim that goes to the very heart of the relationship between library web services and their corporate Internet counterparts and competitors. In an age of hype, information glut, misinformation, start-ups, vertical integration, and dot-com fallout, libraries have relied mainly on their authority, cost-consciousness, substance over form, altruism, consistency, and longevity. It is a righteous stance, but increasingly untenable in the Internet information age. Regardless of personal or professional opinions about the information age and the challenges it presents to libraries, careful analysis and tracking of Internet information providers are practically mandatory for information technology, public services, and technical services staff. Like it or not, the private sector has raised the bar for information access; it is up to libraries to determine whether they will raise it higher, or pass under it without noticing.

WHAT YAHOO DID

When Demetrius Phalereus was sent to Alexandria by Ptolemy Soter to establish a library, he had a clear idea of his goal—to establish an intellectual setting around a collection of manuscripts which would rival that of Athens, a goal worthy of a student of Aristotle. At its height, the library at Alexandria probably contained a copy of every known manuscript in the ancient Greco-Roman world. When we study the surviving legacy of the ancient masters of philosophy, science, history, mathematics, astronomy, and the arts, we sample only a fraction of the works that were preserved and studied at the great Alexandrian library.

When David Filo and Jerry Yang began browsing the World Wide Web as a diversion from their doctoral research at Stanford University, their goals could not compare with those of the architect at Alexandria, but what they built, "Jerry and David's Guide to the World Wide Web"—ultimately, Yahoo—might be called the first Alexandrian catalog of the Web. Despite the economic roller-coaster endured by all Internet-based companies, Yahoo's brand recognition and steadfast popularity have helped maintain its dominant market presence. When librarians think of famous libraries, they think of Alexandria; when the public thinks of Internet guides, it thinks of Yahoo. Yahoo has many things going for it, not the least of which are an easily recalled name and URL, both of which helped the fledgling company in the early days of the Internet. Moreover, Yahoo offered a simple organizing scheme for Internet resources, and was one of the first to apply such organization to an organism that would soon grow faster than anyone could classify it. The subject organization begun by several companies, and mastered by Yahoo, remains a popular way to find Internet resources. The foregoing brief history, however, is not intended to favor Yahoo over the many other organizational websites that are out there. It is the popularity of Yahoo's offerings that should be of interest to libraries, not necessarily Yahoo itself.

Librarians have traditionally (as much as libraries can have "web traditions") found solace in the Tower of Babel that web entrepreneurs have inadvertently created in trying to organize the contents of the Web. Professional cries have run the gamut from "It cannot be done!" or "It should not be done!" to "Only we can do it" and "It cannot be done without us." Others slyly grinned while glancing at the four (now five) large red books of Library of Congress Subject Headings (LCSH), the most comprehensive and arcane organization of resources next to, of course, the Library of Congress classification system itself. But because professional self-righteousness does not mean much in an online environment, we must explore why the new model of resource organization created by Internet entrepreneurs has succeeded and why it maintains its popularity.

"I'm Just Looking, Thanks"

Mention closing the stacks in most academic libraries and you're asking for trouble, if not from your public services staff, then certainly from your faculty. The truth is, users like to browse, and until the advent of the Web, this activity had rarely been replicated in an electronic environment. In the online catalog environment, browsing the old cards was technologically sacrificed for the long-anticipated (and poorly developed over the last decade) advent of the keyword search. That one could flip through cards like scanning the books on a shelf was completely lost on the designers of the first online catalog, and searching for known items remained the online catalog's raison d'être.

When it came to tools like Yahoo, however, so little was known about the Web's rapidly multiplying contents that browsing was the only logical alternative to searching. Rather than establish a controlled vocabulary to describe what existed, the original "Jerry's Bookmarks" were simply links to sites, around which began to grow both a hierarchical and faceted classification scheme. Yahoo would lead its users down paths to resources, rather than expecting them to know where to look. When the Web began its seemingly geometric growth in the mid-1990s, search engines presented themselves as a viable alternative to browsing, but as the usability expert Jakob Nielsen contends, "In reality, search is one of the most common and one of the least successful ways that users look for things on the Web."[1] The major engines that started with simply a search box—mainly AltaVista and Google—learned quickly that searching is not enough and sought to add browsing to their repertoire. But while some services were looking for some sort of browsing capability, those already using it were beginning to see it for the untenable monster that it was. No single company, regardless of how many librarians it hired, could keep up with describing literally billions of web pages. (In the mid-1990s, Yahoo and librarians alike made a big deal of the fact that several professional librarians worked at Yahoo.) One group would take a cue from libraries' cooperative endeavors by forming DMOZ, the Open Directory Project (ODP; www.dmoz.org, now owned by Netscape Communications), which began a cooperative classification project for Internet resources. (See figure 2-1.) Now registered experts provide selective links for various subject categories. The DMOZ structure is then shared with several sites that integrate browsing capabilities into their websites. The following list is just a representative sample of the more than 100 sites that use the ODP cooperative classification system:

AOL Search	Google Directory
Ask Jeeves	HotBot
Biz.com	Lycos
Dictionary.com	Netscape Search
Fansites.com	TotalSeek

Keyword searching will continue to be popular on the Web, but for the most part, such searching entails the pursuit of a single page; queries are not sophisticated, and the vast majority of results returned are not relevant to the user. Browsing via a controlled vocabulary—whether initiated by the user, or suggested by the system, for example, by clicking on a subject heading in a bibliographic record—offers more control, accurate results, and eliminates

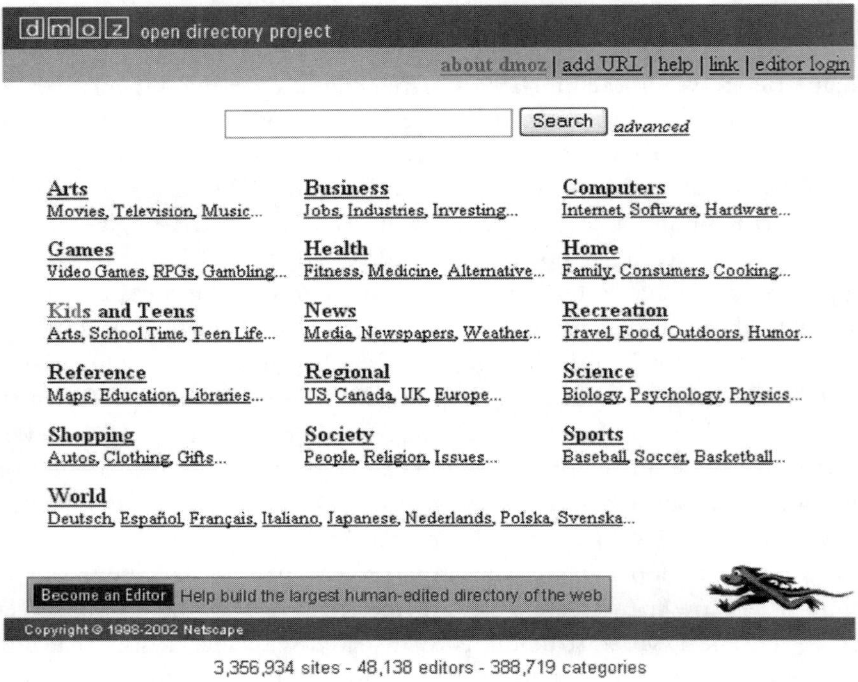

FIGURE 2-1   Netscape website. © 2002 Netscape Communications Corporation. Screenshot used with permission.

information overload. Users find comfort, even if subconsciously, in the controlled nature of browsing, since it adds authority to the search. Another advantage of browsing is that it does not require any typing on the part of the user. Determining which term to use and learning arcane search syntaxes are not an issue when users are presented with user-friendly, clickable, browsing headings.

Online Browsing in Libraries

Now, generally speaking, research libraries like to think of themselves on the cutting edge of services, but the tip of the hat really belongs to both public libraries and vendors when it comes to offering browsing services to their patrons. Exposing themselves to much (undeserved) criticism, several public libraries have modeled their web services on Yahoo subject browsing. Choosing a familiar and easy-to-use interface over the moral outcry of colleagues, several bold libraries chose instant usability rather than bemoaning the popularity of a classification system not created for or by libraries. (See figure 2-2.)

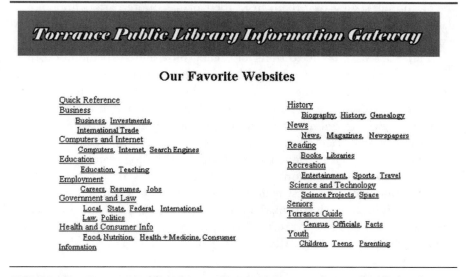

FIGURE 2-2   Torrance Public Library redesigned its gateway to resemble familiar Internet search portals. © 2002, Torrance Public Library. All rights reserved.

Academic libraries would soon follow suit with a more cautious slide down the slippery slope of categorizing electronic resources. Realizing that a browsable list of the LCSH was still beyond their reach, but determined to create categories that satisfied the professional inklings of subject classifications, libraries began creating web pages whose goal was to guide users through a subject maze to a small percentage of their collections, and to even larger piles of web resources that the libraries themselves had already deemed unworthy of cataloging. This cautious move would spark debate on library e-mail lists, at various professional conferences, and in the library literature until the question of how to create these subject lists *automatically* would overshadow further debate on whether or why they should be created at all. Technology in libraries seems no longer a means to an end, but an end in and of itself.

Even this author's library has these subject listings of electronic resources, so what is the problem? Well, simply put, libraries are creating yet another controlled (and contrived) vocabulary for a mere portion of their collections. In the early years of library automation, libraries eagerly added electronic resources to subject guides that contained mostly traditional print resources, but the reverse is hardly true now that electronic resources are so readily available. Most libraries have finally decided to catalog the online resources, but they continue segregating them from their print counterparts. Thousands of databases now exist across libraryland, attempting to provide subject access to electronic resources. But what about the catalog?

Librarians have come to think of catalog browsing as the ability to perform an author, title, or subject search. These searches, however, merely browse authorized indexes and are not truly *browsable* since they all must begin with a keyed search. In what can only be described as an ironic—yet fortunate—twist in online catalog development, major integrated library system vendors have tried quite successfully to create the first truly browsable online catalogs by tying canned, or preformatted, catalog searches to graphical or textual representations of those searches. This is ironic because it arguably empowers the most technical savvy segment of our Internet population, children; and it is fortunate in that it gives libraries a model on which to base future online catalog services not just for children, but also for seniors learning the technology for the first time or for undergraduates learning to use libraries for the first time.

Whether packaged as "featured lists" of new books (titles), recent Caldecott honor winners (authors), or hot topics (subjects), the ability to "can" a catalog search and present it to web users is a simple yet important service for libraries to provide. Moreover, the process itself, assuming that it eventually drops the user in the online catalog, can enhance library pedagogy by clearly presenting to the user what has just occurred and increasing the chance that the user might learn how to perform an actual search. Though there are several ILS examples out there, this screen shot from Innovative Interfaces' KidsOnline is representative of a browsable catalog. (See figure 2-3.)

It should not be lost on the reader that creating these features does mean more work on the part of catalogers, subject specialists, and (depending on the features of one's online catalog) IT professionals. Perhaps this is the major distinction between what Yahoo originally intended in creating its bookmarks

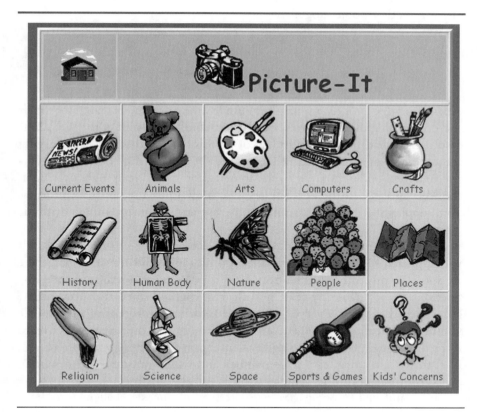

FIGURE 2-3   Innovative Interfaces' KidsOnline uses graphic images to browse the library's holdings. © 2002, Innovative Interfaces. All rights reserved.

and what Yahoo learned when it tried to categorize immense piles of content—selection, subject specialties, and scholarship.

Upon further reflection, the comparison of Yahoo to the Alexandrian library might miss its mark. The traditional bibliotheca—like Alexandria's predecessor in Athens—might seem more appropriate. *Scholarship* distinguished Alexandria from its contemporaries, and the same should be true of the distinction between Yahoo and library websites, between Internet data filers and librarians. The Web cannot be thought of as scholarship in and of itself; it is a guide, a set of pointers, a pile of content unmatched by anything else in history. Tools like the DMOZ organization and sophisticated search algorithms are just that—tools. True web scholarship will be defined by how libraries apply web strategies to the traditional aspects of their missions. But this book is about libraries and business; the topic of librarians and scholars is one for another book altogether.

DO YOU GOOGLE?

Librarians place a lot of emphasis on both learning how users search for things and on teaching them how to search better. Until the advent of the Web, database queries had been the purview of professionals and a few experts, with the advanced query structure of Dialog and OCLC serving as keys to the elusive untamed pile of content in the information castle. Seemingly overnight, the Web disregarded the key-holders and threw open the doors to information, supplanting (and diminishing) expertise and accuracy with algorithmic prowess.

Like it or not, Internet search engines have forever changed how users will approach searching for information on a topic. And like it or not, there are some lessons to be learned from how search engines serve users, and distinctions to be made between how search engines work and how online library searches work. Everyone has their favorite search engine, but Google will be used here as representative of the Internet search engine collective; to its credit, though, Google also deserves attention for coming up with a brand label that is fun to say, easy to remember, and which can serve as both noun and verb in relation to its function.

In a nutshell, Google has presented an immense challenge to both libraries and library automation vendors. It is difficult, if not impossible, to explain to the average undergraduate or public library user why Google can search *billions* of web pages faster than an online catalog or journal article index can search *millions* of surrogate records. It is hardly worth our professional time to explain that web indexing that is one to five years old is infinitely superior to indexing methods created by integrated library system vendors ten to twenty years ago; users don't (nor should they) care. ILS vendors that are not working on new methods to index old records will be forever lost in an Internet culture that rewards instant gratification with return visits.

MARC Is Dead! Long Live MARC

Moreover, returning accurate results quickly in easy-to-learn ways is hardly just a public services issue. Library catalogers have expressed mixed reactions to the new prominence of XML (extensible markup language) and its relationship to the MARC format. Dick R. Miller, systems librarian and head of technical services at the Lane Medical Library at Stanford, explains: "The core of libraries' data troves are stored in proprietary formats of integrated library systems (ILS) and in the complex and arcane MARC formats—both restricted chiefly to the province of technical services and systems librarians."[2] Libraries may have already noticed that search engines like Google have mastered indexing PDF documents for inclusion in search results. How long before MARC records are next? With a finite number of library automation vendors and a finite number of library systems, how long before Google builds itself the one-stop library? MARC's context is as difficult to explain to researchers—and just plain searchers—as are antiquated index algorithms. If XML is truly the Internet flavor of the future, and libraries hope to conduct their business online, then MARC itself deserves serious redress, or at the very least, a level of attention equal to that afforded by libraries' corporate counterparts.

What does Google teach libraries, then? At the very least, it teaches all web service providers that users expect fast and simple access to indexed surrogate records. A simple search box and an advanced algorithm prove nearly as successful as an authorized heading search or complex Boolean query. None of this is meant to advocate the death of MARC. The fact remains that library vendors support it quite well, and the profession has devoted countless hours and unlimited devotion to its support and development. What XML offers, however, is a middle ground that might appease both a cataloger's sense of organization and a user's expectation of quick and simple displays of needed information. For example, XML applications such as the Encoded

Archival Initiative (EAD) for describing archival finding aids and resources place XML in a library context *and* address a need that the MARC record has not. MARC proves inadequate as a surrogate for most archival records, and XML does well, both as descriptor and as markup for the resource itself.

Every Surfer His Web Page

This bad play on the words of S. R. Ranganathan best describes the warped sense of positive feedback that search engines like Google have made users come to expect. Google's attention to "fuzzy matching"—the ability to reformulate searches and present alternatives for presupposed anticipated results—borders on devotion. "Sometimes, 'NO TITLES FOUND' is the answer," was the astute observation of Karen Ciccone, head of the Natural Resources Library, when a group of librarians debated the display of search results screens for the online catalog at North Carolina State University Libraries. On the Web, there is a concerted effort among search engines to always return *something*. Seemingly starved for positive feedback, users might expect any number of links to resources that a librarian would quickly consider a "false drop" in a database search. The challenge, then, for libraries and their information vendors is twofold: incorporate the best components of positive feedback (or fuzzy matching) and educate users about the precision and authority of library searching and resources, respectively. This topic will be addressed further in chapter 3.

Not all dot-com solutions present themselves as complements to library services. Some are simply commercial services for which the library has no truly equivalent service, such as full web searching, discussion lists, indexes of mixed format or ephemeral materials, and book and music purchases. This does not preclude libraries, however, from learning lessons based on the service models that these corporations have created. The next three sections of this chapter will take a detailed look at three of these services—online reference, content delivery, and online bookstores.

ASK JEEVES OR LIVEPERSON
The Dot-com Reference Desk

One of the unintended barriers of library service is the traditional reference desk. When it was the only place to go for authoritative information referrals, it was a hurdle that most people would overcome. When libraries offered alternatives, like the online catalog, finding aids, and browsable collections of electronic resources, users faced new barriers of professional organization, controlled vocabularies, and klunky search interfaces. When the Internet began to offer alternatives, users flocked to them for their speed and simplicity. When the search engines began to offer natural language search options, to many, the syllogism was complete and both the physical and virtual library space suffered for it.

Just Ask Anyone

Despite what some would call a firm embrace of technology by the general library community, reliance on the physical brick and mortar of libraries remains an important distinction in an information economy where URLs change as quickly as dot-com CEOs, and virtual spaces are as fleeting as startup venture capital. Even this profession's so-called digital libraries have physical locations, usually within the walls of the traditional building still called "the library." Daniel Greenstein, head of the California Digital Library, writing with Jerry George, reminds us that "Digital libraries are not separate institutions paralleling traditional libraries; instead, they are collections that apply new technologies to the historical role of libraries as stewards of our cultural heritage."[3] But more than just brick and mortar, libraries distinguish themselves by the human touch that comes with providing information resources, reference advice, and readers' services to patrons from all walks of life. Surely, this distinction would be safe from the Internet. Or so libraries thought.

Digital Information Servants

"Digital information servant" is really just a generic code phrase for Ask Jeeves, the most widely known "artificial intelligence" agent on the Web. Ask Jeeves.com (AJ) offers the ability to phrase questions in natural language. The AJ software then translates the request into several alternatives from which users can choose to submit their question more authoritatively. AJ is not the only search engine that handles natural language queries, but the way that most others do so is to strip irrelevant words from the query and use other sophisticated algorithms to try to figure out what the searcher is getting at. This form of natural language capability, however, is still better than that offered in every online library catalog and most index, abstract, and full-text databases.

For a while this solution sufficed, but it was only a matter of time before users would miss the personal touch they once had from information professionals; many users, however, had already forgotten where that personal touch used to come from. Luckily for the new dot-coms, a solution was already at hand.

Personal Information Servants

Somehow, people's opinions take on new authority when viewed in print or on a website. Say what you will about the artificial intelligence and algorithmic nature of searching for information on the Web, the latest trend is personalized service, customized to users' needs. Someone finally figured out (or caught up to librarians' notions, as the case may be) that people could be classified by subject in the same way that resources are. This would allow Internet sites to allow access to actual humans with claims of expertise in certain subject areas.

As the technical hurdles became smaller—more broadband Internet access, better file compression, and a chat-savvy web community—dot-coms began to see the potential of adding a human touch to their virtual e-commerce space. This electronic foray into customer relationship management (CRM) software would take the e-commerce industry by storm, and libraries by surprise. Four leading players in the field, LivePerson, WebHelp, KANA, and eGain, boast the best solutions for electronically communicating with online customers. All four offer some version of chat software and co-browsing (the ability to take control of a remote user's web browser) capabilities. This sudden panacea has placed a new premium on human contact in the traditional customer service model that was, until this era, steadily replaced with web FAQs, knowledge bases, and recorded phone menuing systems.

LivePerson was one of the first real-time customer-service chat services on the net. (See figure 2-4.) Long before its availability, though, libraries around the world had used chat services to communicate with each other or with patrons. Services like LivePerson, however, not only added the component of co-browsing—the ability to walk a user through a website—but also made libraries aware that another commercial venture might compete with traditional library services. Libraries around the world are now scrambling to establish some sort of "virtual reference" or reference chat service. But there is more to learn here than just a new service. Libraries should not only mimic the innovative services offered by Internet companies, they should constantly position themselves to capitalize on the shortcomings of the very services they hope to emulate.

FIGURE 2-4   An interactive session with LivePerson. © 2002, LivePerson.
All rights reserved.

For those who have ever used an online help desk, the service might well
be described as virtual, unless the most basic of questions is the focus. (Let's
face it, library humans are better than help desk humans.) Libraries, on the
other hand, manage everything from simple questions to complex reference
queries; and they do this in person, by e-mail, by phone, and online. (See figure 2-5.) Calling these services "virtual reference," however, does a disservice
to both the technology and the people that operate it. As oxymoronic as "virtual reality," virtual reference should be redefined as "digital reference."
Moreover, calling the service something simple like "chat" might help market
the service to undergraduates and high school students, even though the service itself should be thought of as much more than that.

The best thing that libraries could hope for in online reference tools is
happening as well. This is the repackaging and redistribution of online packages such as eGain by library specialists like Library Services and Systems,
LLC (LSSI). While this product in particular will be discussed in more detail
later, libraries can breathe a collective sigh of relief at the automation-library
partnerships that are emerging around online reference services. High-
tech/high-touch will be of particular concern to libraries for the next several
years, and libraries are best positioned to supply both.

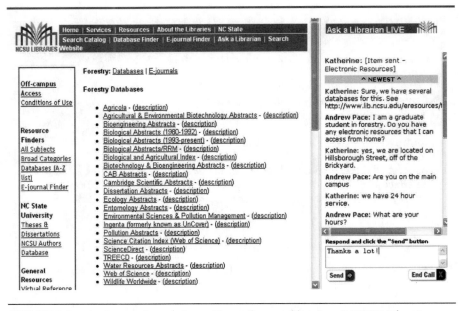

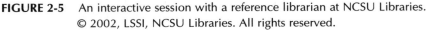

FIGURE 2-5   An interactive session with a reference librarian at NCSU Libraries.

CONTENTVILLE . . . WE DELIVER

Technology and interface design are a lot easier to talk about than actual content. Selling content on the Internet has proven to be a real challenge for most dot-coms, and severely distinguishes the corporate retail mission from a library's goal of inexpensive and efficient content distribution. Moreover, tracking dot-com information retailers is a lot like shooting at a moving (and often disappearing) target. In fact, an interesting thing happened while this author was writing about content. Contentville, an information reseller, went out of business. As glad (as a librarian) as I am at the demise of a pay service that most citizens should enjoy for free, it is almost sad to see this competition expire before it could be made clear that libraries—and Contentville's own ignorance—defeated it. Contentville emerged at the height of the dot-com boom. Convinced through osmosis and never-ending media coverage that America is now an information economy, companies like Contentville, ebrary, and others rushed to amass digital content and the ability to access it at a frantic pace. However, these companies didn't stop to consider the fact that the United States' economy is based on information about as much as it is based on individual dollar bills. Discrete pieces of information have about as much bearing on an economy as the money in one's own pocket. Piles of money (information?), well managed (knowledge?) and earning interest (wisdom?), on the other hand, present a whole new picture, and help explain the failure of companies like Contentville.

Why then be sad at their demise? There is an important reason. It can generally be said (this author is not a market analyst or even a business expert) that the venture capital behind most Internet start-ups has gone into technology. Human intellectual resources should have been part of that investment, but Internet start-ups (especially failed ones) bank on two assumptions: (1) intellectual capital is far more expensive than technical infrastructure, and (2) technical infrastructure and good web design are suitable substitutes for intellectual capital. The very nature of commercial web services can be described as an effort to replace intellectual capital with technology. What a company like Contentville brings to the mix, then, is really cool technology. Strip the cool layers off the (with hindsight) rather vacuous content, and one is left with something that might look like a library web page for a library with no books and no librarians. The danger lies in being too quick to celebrate the demise of Contentville's business model based on its poor content. Libraries have good content and less technology. Imagine good content combined with great technology, and then tell your library recruiters that a few hundred former dot-commers are hitting the street and looking for work. (See chapter 3 for more on Contentville and the fallout of its recent demise in the dot-com bust.)

There's a saying—modified depending on taste—that goes around the business, academic, and public services world. When it comes to service, the saying goes: Quick, Thorough, Cheap . . . pick two. By adapting the service model of the dot-com information providers, like the defunct Contentville, libraries could be poised to deliver all three. More aptly described as "deliveryville," Contentville's essential problem was that it did not have the content. Libraries, on the other hand, face the problem of not having the Internet service model or technology to step up to the plate. By paying close attention to the Internet service models and technology of dot-coms, libraries have a lot to gain. People are after information; libraries have it and the expertise required to distinguish one piece of it from another. Libraries are the true contentville. If America truly *is* an information economy, then libraries are the gold standard behind it.

THE AMAZONIAN CATALOG

If any Internet company has raised the bar for libraries, it is Amazon.com. Unlike most competition, however, this was never really the intention of Amazon, which aimed to capture a portion of the disposable income that just so happens to belong to those who also use libraries (just take a look at the cars in the parking lot of the average public library). That librarians continue to bemoan the breadth and reach of a company that puts books in the hands of readers smells of sour grapes. Despite Amazon's seeming inability to turn a profit, its popularity continues, and its name has become synonymous with buying books online. But rather than feel camaraderie at the book-pusher's inability to make reading profitable—isn't this one of the main reasons we have lending libraries?—libraries take the moral high ground, firm in the belief that information wants to be free. The profession's resistance to Amazon has achieved levels rarely seen in libraries' traditional relationship with brick-and-mortar bookstores.

It would seem to the casual (or, in this case, passionate) observer that jealousy is at the heart of viewing Amazon as a competitor. This company pursues the library market with reckless abandon, cheap prices, and a feature-driven website that is more style than substance. If the Internet economy has made one thing clear, however, it is that style draws the audience and substance keeps it coming back. Isn't it time for libraries to get past petty jealousies and begin the process of emulating (stealing, if you will) the style that has made the Web so famous? What, then, do we have to learn from Amazon?

MARC vs. Books in Print

MARC is what is there, so MARC is the format libraries use when organizing their catalog databases. Amazon.com, however, would not venture down this path—selling is its goal, not thorough description by use of an increasingly arcane system. The *Books in Print* database would serve as the groundwork for Amazon's online database of books; it would add value—reviews, book jackets, excerpts, etc.—to the records as it went along. (See figure 2-6.) After nearly twenty years of mainstream library automation, one of the purest ironies is libraries' unswerving devotion to the MARC format. Even though ILS companies rely on the minutia of MARC less and less, libraries continue to engage in the exactness of cataloging, which is arguably the closest thing to science in library science. For example, how many online catalogs take full advantage of the MARC leader? Does the online catalog recognize a record

FIGURE 2-6   Amazon.com title display. This is only part of an enriched record display that also includes reviews, customer reviews, links to similar titles, and Library of Congress Subject Heading terms.
© 2002, courtesy of Amazon.com, Inc. All rights reserved.

as a periodical because position 21 of the 008 field is a "p"? Are multiple formats recognized in the 006 field? Even outside the minutia of the 00X fields, how many library automation companies have embraced the Library of Congress's long-awaited changes to the formatting of the 856 field for descriptions of online resources?

This is not intended to start a philosophical war of words on the value of cataloging. Right now, it is practically the only thing libraries have to work with in organizing access to their resources. Long before Amazon, libraries struggled to add value to MARC records through added titles, local subject headings, call number browsing, and finally, tables of contents. ILS vendors, faithfully trying to do their part to make the standard flexible, offered various indexing options based on the fields in the bibliographic record. But in the twenty-first century, and with Amazon as a comparative model, adding more content to a MARC record is much like trying to get a square peg through a round hole. The relational database model coupled with the distributed computing model of the Web now allows libraries and vendors alike to add value to bibliographic and holdings displays without creating a MARC record in danger of collapsing under its own weight.

Push Marketing

The term "push marketing" sounds like something that traditional libraries did for decades, that is, when professional librarians (or even just readers) worked the circulation desk and helped patrons select titles from the shelf: "If you like this, then you'll certainly like this as well." Not content to simply count sales for the mere sake of a number on a spreadsheet, Amazon decided to capture and use the data collected from its patrons in order to market other titles to them. Moreover, recommendations could be made based on what other people picked when they bought a particular title. Aside from the temptation to lead fellow consumers astray with one's own eclectic tastes, the feature is intriguing, if not successful. The notion of applying this feature to a library environment, however, is met immediately with cries of privacy protection, and a strong desire to erase that sort of user data lest some law enforcement agency impel the library to give it up. The issue of privacy will be addressed again in chapter 7; suffice it to say that libraries' strict adherence to privacy protection will require them to abjure some of the features inherently possible in an online environment.

A Piece of the Action

One of the latest Amazon.com features to hit the Web enables the average consumer to capitalize on Amazon's immense catalog and its captive market. Users can now make their own books available for used book prices. The seller provides all the data about the book and performs all shipping; Amazon receives a sizable portion of the profit simply for providing the interface. It has always struck this author as odd that libraries go to the trouble of actually withdrawing titles from the online catalog, eradicating their existence both physically and virtually, only to attempt to sell them on a browsable shelf. Why not sell the title directly from the catalog? Why not solicit purchases the same way? Simply put, libraries do not want to present themselves as commercial enterprises (some state institutions are even strictly prohibited from doing so).

The World's Largest Library

The librarian and writer Steve Coffman asked—not so rhetorically—why librarians could not build the world's largest library by applying Amazonian qualities to both the online library catalog and interlibrary lending policies.[4] Libraries are slowed and constrained by their nonprofit status, their decentralized nature, and a sense of competition that applies to other libraries, but not to the private sector. Even the simplest aspect of Amazon's business model seems beyond the reach of the average library. In a survey conducted by the NCSU Libraries' MyLibrary Management Committee, one candid comment from a user captured the attention of those who dream of seeing the library compete with dot-coms. The sentiment expressed is paraphrased here: "I don't use the library portal as much as I used to since I started using Amazon. I would stay with Amazon if for no other reason than it delivers the material I need directly to my door."

Not all libraries and ILS vendors would sit idly by while Amazon and its ilk captured feature possibilities that OPACs had ignored for two decades (the specifics of some of these features are discussed in the next chapter). The careful application of dot-com Internet solutions will not blur the line between the public and private sectors—book lenders and booksellers serve different purposes. This does not mean, however, that libraries must provide free services with boring or valueless interfaces. Library catalogs can become more than mere inventories, built to tell their users the location of a title. If libraries wish to meet the expectations of their users beyond their traditional framework, there are lessons to be learned from the Internet's for-profit sector.

All of the concepts discussed in this chapter—browsing, searching, asking, delivering, and adding value—are hardly features invented by Internet businesses. One might argue, however, that dot-coms have established themselves as the new standard bearers for innovation in information access and distribution. Yahoo, Google, and Amazon probably have nothing to fear from libraries; but the reverse may not be true. These Internet upstarts represent a phenomenon that sheds unwelcome light on a library's complacency, its desire to return to a service model where "free" was good enough, where expertise was unquestioned and unavailable from other sources. That Yahoo mastered web browsing, or that Amazon has done more with a simple *Books in Print* index in five years than libraries and their vendors did in over twenty, should not bring shame upon the profession; but neither should it give rise to professional guile. The bar has been raised, and it is time for libraries to reach for it rather than stare up at it.

Notes

1. Jakob Nielsen, *Designing Web Usability* (Indianapolis: New Riders, 2000).
2. Dick R. Miller, "XML: Libraries' Strategic Opportunity," *Library Journal Netconnect* (2000): 18–22.
3. Daniel Greenstein and Jerry George, "Building a Library Service Network," *CLIR Issues,* no. 23 (2001): 3–7.
4. Steven Coffman, "Building the World's Largest Library: Driving the Future," *Searcher* 7, no. 3 (1999): 34–37. See also Coffman, "The Response to 'Building the World's Largest Library,'" *Searcher* 7, no. 7 (1999): 28–32.

3 | BUSINESS CHALLENGES TO LIBRARY PRACTICES

It's disintermediation, and the library is the odd man out.

—Mick O'Leary

THE COMMERCIALIZATION OF LIBRARY SERVICES

It sounds like a made-up word, but "disintermediation" is the new information buzzword that supposedly threatens library services. The commercialization of library services is as old as information broker services, which predate the Web by several decades. Easy access to the Web, however, has made libraries nervous at the same rate that it has provided some Internet start-ups with millions in venture capital. Had libraries been as quick to patent the interlibrary loan business model as Amazon.com was in patenting one-click shopping, the millions in royalties might have made libraries rich enough to buy out the online competition. This chapter will take a look at several moderately successful ventures that have tried to replace, augment, or disintermediate library services. Finally, it will examine how several digital library services are already adopting some of the strategies and technology brought to the table by upstart start-ups. Libraries are indeed positioned to "re-intermediate" themselves into a market that they still dominate, and which they will ultimately control in the meantime. Information is hot, and libraries should position themselves as close to the flame as possible without getting burned.

Library-in-a-Box: Questia

Libraries set the stage with the online catalog and various periodical indexes, the first in a series of electronically available resources that would whet users' appetites for instant gratification. Full-text resources would soon follow, including full electronic journals, and eventually the electronic book. Digitization projects would add thousands of resources, and even digitally born, or "electronic only," resources would appear on the scene in several libraries. The problem, like that besetting the original nonintegrated modular library systems, is that all of these resources come in parts, with the library responsible for integrating them into a cohesive suite of digital services. Some libraries have tried to centralize control through use of the online catalog, but the changing nature of online resources—URLs, coverage dates, changing suppliers, and other elements—makes this sort of data too difficult to easily control in traditional online catalogs. It was only a matter of time before some corporate interest created the "library-in-a-box" concept that would integrate varied content under one umbrella, even a small umbrella.

If not first, then certainly the best known, Questia attempts to be the solution that every undergraduate with even the mildest case of bibliophobia will embrace. (See appendix A for a description of this and other companies discussed in this book.) Questia wants to make itself into the ultimate one-stop shopping point for everyone seeking a least common denominator solution to their information needs. What Questia and its ilk lack in content, they more than make up for in value-added interfaces and marketing strategies. One of the first to market itself directly to students (and their parents), Questia, who will not disclose the number of subscribers it has, now boasts access to over 70,000 book and journal articles in the humanities and social sciences, and a staff of 25 with one professional librarian (these last two numbers are in sharp decline compared to their start-up figures, which could mark the beginning of the end for Questia). The threat comes in destabilizing the status quo relationship that libraries and book vendors have enjoyed for over a century. By making deals directly with publishers, Questia removes the library as intermediary for the delivery of content to the end-user.

This new model even supplants the highly praised library model presented by netLibrary, in which libraries purchase or lease titles, and circulation is based on a single-user access to any title purchased, which is easily equitable with printed book circulation. While it is difficult for most librarians to discuss Questia without editorializing on philosophical (or hurt feelings') grounds, this section will attempt, somewhat objectively, to deconstruct Questia and other services like it, current and future.

Philosophy

After drawing some initial backlash from libraries, including some criticism of librarians who had joined its ranks as staff or advisors (a new dark side . . . sound familiar?), Questia has attempted to reposition itself as an online complement to libraries:

> The Questia service is an online library focusing on the humanities and social sciences. However, our service is not designed to be a substitute for a traditional library but rather is designed to make an extensive collection of titles and research tools available online to students 24 hours a day, 7 days a week. We believe that physical libraries, and their librarians, will continue to play a key role in the future of research and education.[1]

This sentiment is less clear, however, in Questia's marketing campaign, which paints the physical library in a less flattering light. (See figure 3-1.) Questia attempts to be hip by speaking the language of the average undergraduate, and by making pleas that appeal to those with habits like procrastination, laziness, and the need for instant gratification.

OTHER INTERNET SOURCES	QUESTIA'S ONLINE LIBRARY
Lots of junk to filter through	Scholarly books and journal articles selected by librarians
Only abstracts and summaries	Complete books cover to cover - read or search any page or all of the book
Professor won't accept www.joebob's website as a source	Credible sources from hundreds of respected publishers
Sifting through 4,795 websites affects your social calendar	Just visit one library - Questia - to complete your research in no time at all
Slave over formatting of bibliographies	Exclusive tools that create your footnotes and bibliography quickly

TRADITIONAL LIBRARY	QUESTIA'S ONLINE LIBRARY
Closes nightly	Open 24 hours a day, 7 days a week
Late fees, books checked out for weeks	Books never checked out and no overdue fees
Need change for the copier	Print pages for free
Not allowed to mark book pages	Go ahead, highlight and scribble on our pages
Keeping track of your sources is a nightmare	Automatically records sources used and creates bibliography

FIGURE 3-1   Questia marketing campaign: physical library complement, or competition? © 2002, Questia, Inc. All rights reserved.

Features

What Questia overstates in its marketing campaign it more than makes up for with a feature-rich online catalog environment. The first feature that distinguishes it from a traditional catalog, of course, is the presence of full text. (See figure 3-2.) This full text is searchable throughout the database. Questia will also take users directly to pages on which it finds search terms. The search engine proves quirky at times, but the same could be said of most library catalogs. Among the most notable features are the ability to re-search within search results, highlight text, add notes to text, and paste citations and footnotes directly into word processing programs. How helpful these features are to users is undetermined; that these features do not exist in most library interfaces is undeniable.

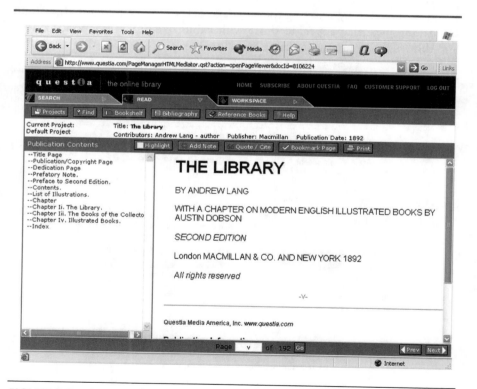

FIGURE 3-2   An example of a Questia online resource. © 2002, Questia, Inc.
            All rights reserved.

Questia also offers the ability to browse its collection with a variety of broad subject headings. This searchless interface is intriguing, and for a collection of limited size, like Questia's, allows users to wade into the holdings without coming up empty-handed, as most novice attempts at Library of Congress Subject Headings searches do. The most enviable of all its features, however, are Questia's 24 x 7 availability and its multiuser access policy. These two features distinguish it from most library print collections and electronic collections such as netLibrary, which still support only a single user for each title purchased.

Content

Questia opened its digital doors in January 2001 with 35,000 digital books. That total has not increased much in the year since its inception, and Questia is already falling far short of its goal to have 250,000 titles by 2003. An economic downturn, which forced the layoff of several staff, has also slowed production. The firm's founder and CEO, Troy Williams, began with the hope that Questia might serve as a great equalizer for liberal arts content; if, by some miracle, Questia does reach its self-imposed goal of 250,000 titles, its collection would be larger than those of 80 percent of all U.S. academic libraries.[2] Unfortunately, the number of volumes is not the only thing that counts; quantity means nothing without quality. Besides being almost completely devoted to the humanities and social sciences—Questia has hedged on plans to release more science and business titles—a close look at publishing dates and coverage reveals large collection gaps.

Susan Gibbons, a librarian at the University of Rochester who is also director of the LSTA-funded Ebook Evaluation Project and Digital Initiatives, is the first to provide an in-depth look at the collection status of Questia. A random sampling of 100 monographs had an average publication date of 1973, with only one title published after 1999. Questia attributes the age of its collection to an emphasis on seminal texts, but the retrospective value of these nonfiction texts is limited. A similar sampling of online articles, added in April 2001, showed that the majority were published between 1994 and 1998, with an average publication date of 1994.[3] Questia's collection development, which is still based primarily on demand, is haphazard by most library standards, which is why the company relies on the somewhat disingenuous defense that the collection is meant merely to complement existing brick-and-mortar library collections.

Service

Despite Questia's least common denominator collection base, it is still a one-size-fits-all solution. While the user is somewhat trapped within its framework in order to use its features, there is no need to make distinctions between index, abstract, and full text, or between HTML, PDF, and ASCII. These distinctions, which are often lost on patrons, do not exist in Questia's library-in-a-box. Gibbons concludes that as long as library collections remain relevant and vital, Questia is not really a threat to library service; it is, however, a threat to the quality of resources offered to students and faculty.[4] The tone, language, frequency, and breadth of its advertising messages do threaten to drown out the relative silence of most libraries which have not decided whether to acquiesce, retreat, or fight when facing this new challenge.

Pay-by-the-Drink: Ebrary

A slight twist on the Questia model, ebrary presents itself as a New Age photocopy machine. The main difference between Questia and ebrary, besides content, is that ebrary does not require an account to search its database. Cutting and pasting from its resources, however, does incur a fee; hence, the analogy of the photocopier. Its CEO and founder, Christopher Warnock, summarizes, "We are not an ebook company . . . We're not a bookseller . . . We are a software company with a killer app[lication]."[5]

Philosophy

Perhaps learning from the mistakes of its predecessors (netLibrary also launched a failed individual subscriber effort in its early stages), ebrary adds a marketing component that benefits all relevant stakeholders. Ebrary offers searching, browsing, *and reading* of its online content. Pay-per-use does not kick in until text is copied or printed from the online resource; the pay-for-use service is run under a debit system that allows users to deposit funds into their account for use of the system. Ebrary's most interesting philosophical departure came when it suggested that everyone, including libraries, get a piece of the action—60 percent to publishers and 5 percent to libraries of the total revenue from activity performed at local terminals. In April 2002, ebrary announced a major shift in this policy, offering libraries unlimited access, with subscription rates based on library type and FTE (full-time equivalent) user base. As it turned out, libraries did not really want a piece of the action, especially from a vendor (go figure). Ebrary now admits that it is probably better that the model failed, since it made the company explore more equitable pricing structures for libraries. The model can still be described as pay-by-the-drink, however, since libraries can choose to either pay the whole cost of copying and printing, or simply subsidize that cost.[6]

By trying to replicate the analog activity of browsing book collections—that is, browse and then pay, like browse and then circulate—rather than copying the activity prescribed by other online information vendors—that is, pay first, and then read, copy, and print—ebrary has hit upon a truly novel business model. Add a killer application like ebrary's web interface to the mix, and you have the second ingredient for a successful business.

Features

Like the adage that says the second mouse gets the cheese, ebrary's adaptations of Questia's feature set is well done. The search engine is faster, the content displayed in a more user-friendly manner, and the features match the integration that patrons are seeking. The fact that users can search and view full text of ebrary's content without buying first is still the most intriguing aspect of its service model, but other features stand out as well. The system highlights full text, and users can jump from hit to hit within a given title. Since the source document is PDF, most of the applicable features of that format are included in the display. (See figure 3-3.)

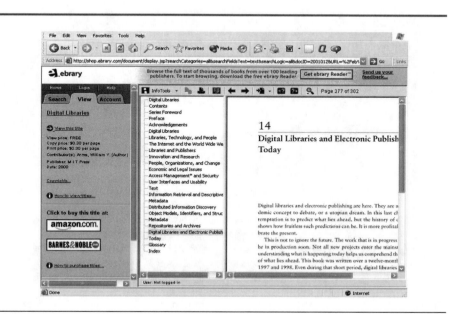

FIGURE 3-3   Ebrary enters the digital library arena. © 2002, ebrary, Inc. All rights reserved.

The InfoTools section (see figure 3-4) allows users to pass searches or specific portions of content to third-party sites. These "channel partners" allow users to translate passages, look up terms in a dictionary or encyclopedia, browse the Web, and purchase the book; moreover, the links to these partners are customizable by libraries, so linking to existing resources which the library is already paying for is also possible.

Content

Ebrary has considerably less content than its fellow e-book distributors, but given a service model that rewards copyright holders to the tune of 60 percent, this is sure to change rapidly. Generally, ebrary's collection of front titles seems more impressive than its competitors, so what it lacks in quantity it seems to be making up for in quality and currency. Although the title list includes many imprints from 2000 and 2001, this can be somewhat misleading, because all public domain classics carry an ebrary imprint; a nonscientific sampling, however, of eighty titles found an average publication date of 1999, which

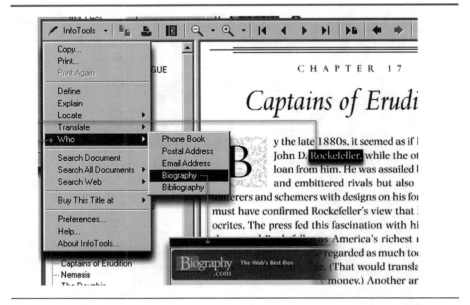

FIGURE 3-4   Ebrary's InfoTools integrates third-party resources into digital library content. © 2002, ebrary, Inc. All rights reserved.

is significantly more recent than the vast majority of Questia's collection.[7] Moreover, since the initial collection does not include much journal material, the content portion could prove more attractive to libraries that already subscribe to many full-text journal resources.

Ebrary's InfoTools also integrates with content that the library has already purchased. This model should be attractive to libraries that do not want to purchase just another stand-alone full-text module for their users. Being able to control which channels are available does pose collection problems, however, since libraries will have to decide on a suite of least common denominator resources from which the ebrary reader will link.

Service

By marketing itself as a library partner and revising its pricing plans to facilitate organizational access, ebrary is putting good faith behind its effort to serve the end-user, without any suspicion surrounding its intentions. Ebrary has also taken lessons from netLibrary in its approach to offering MARC records to libraries that purchase titles. It will be interesting to see whether libraries decide to insert MARC records into their OPACs, since the titles are not really owned. This represents a greater departure for library practice than entering 856 links to resources that are licensed or endorsed by collection managers.

Whether ebrary itself will survive remains to be seen, but as Mick O'Leary points out, these sorts of innovations usually survive to shape new markets.[8] By trying to replicate analog library activity—browsing, reading, photocopying—ebrary may be the first to realistically contribute to a major paradigm shift without the corresponding philosophical fallout.

Full-Service Content Development: XanEdu

Somewhere in between Questia and ebrary lies XanEdu, the "Utopia for the mind," as its marketing logo claims. Created by Bell & Howell, and powered by the content of Proquest databases, XanEdu markets itself first as a service to faculty, and then offers added-value content to their students. XanEdu presents one of the more challenging end-runs around libraries, since the content that is marketed to end-users is wrapped up in a service which many libraries do not have. XanEdu allows faculty to submit course reserve content or syllabi, or allows faculty to create their own custom coursepacks online. Faculty too busy to keep up with the changing literature in their field can also enlist Bell & Howell to update the content for them. By partnering with the online course management giant, Blackboard, XanEdu completes its strategy of cutting out the library middleman and marketing content to users who may already be paying premium dollars for the exact same content, sometimes even from Bell & Howell itself.

As noted, this is a particular challenge to libraries, since the service model creates something that libraries may not be doing, that is, supplying digital access to course readings. Since the guidelines of course reserve materials are built around access to *supplemental* readings, not coursepacks, services like XanEdu put libraries at a disadvantage. Since seamless access to full-text content buried under database front-ends is hidden by many library vendors, tools—even ones that cost users money—that bring that content to light are attractive to end-users. That Bell & Howell is developing this strategy for online access in tandem with its adherence to deep-linking for libraries (the ability to link directly to full text at the article level) seems duplicitous, especially since the XanEdu website issues no warnings about checking with local libraries for licensed access.

Catalog, Content, and Customers: Together at Last?

It's hard to imagine that library technology has come so far so fast. Few predicted the pace at which digital collections, especially e-books, would grow. And while the pace and acceptance of this new medium might best be described as evolutionary, not revolutionary from a publisher's viewpoint, for many libraries, it is world-shattering. For a profession that has had to deal with creating surrogate records for all of its collections, indexes and abstracts for its periodicals, and finding aids for its archival records, the marriage of catalog and content presents troubling, and awe-inspiring, challenges for libraries. This section will assume, for the sake of space, that users want full text; it will ignore, for the sake of retaining readers, the arguments about reading books and articles on computer screens and curling up on beaches with e-books. Digital content is not about reader hardware and software, but about the digitization of content for delivery by whatever mechanism the next brilliant technologist can dream up.

The Walls of the Box

The particular challenge for libraries is to educate users about the walls of digital content that they build up around themselves when deriving content from online vendors, whether access to those resources comes from direct marketing or through library subscription services. In the early days of digital content, the main challenge was to alert users to the vast wealth of print resources that online databases, index and abstract services, and the Web failed to cover. Now dot-com vendors have supplanted that macro view of library content by trimming down digital content even more and packaging it with a broad range of online features, low-cost alternatives, and remote, round-the-clock access. This will be an especially difficult challenge for libraries to face, as convenience counters authority in the age of the Web.

Unfortunately, the sole attempt (outside of libraries, of course) to bring several different types of content under one umbrella died with the dot-com demise of Contentville. Contentville received a lot of flak from the library world for its pedestrian approach to content, but it should have been lauded for its attempts to bring together a great variety of ephemeral content: books, e-books, out-of-print books, screenplays, dissertations, magazines, study guides, speeches, legal documents, and television transcripts. Its founder, Steven Brill, fell victim to his own naiveté about copyright (a poor excuse for a lawyer), and in many ways played the fall guy for an industry concerned about Napster-like transgressions in the text world. Fallout in the wake of the UnCover class action suit, in which authors were recompensated for the sale of articles online, and the Supreme Court's decision in the Tasini case, in which freelance authors successfully sued to retain copyright of digital versions of their work, put the final nails in the coffin of Contentville in the fall of 2001. It's too late now, but libraries might have learned a lot from the cross-collection search capabilities of Contentville, and the packaging and delivery methods of its content shone in comparison to most interlibrary loan delivery models.

Fortunately, another model exists with a market presence that was overshadowed by Contentville's marketing blitz (a blitz that also contributed to the venture's demise, since it garnered a lot of attention). ELibrary combines the business models of Questia (subscription service), Contentville (varied resources), and ebrary (slick design) into one service that predated all three. Though the market is a bit different, mostly secondary education, the model is similar. ELibrary suffers the same content woes of its Internet brethren, but as revenue flows adjust, clear winners will continue to emerge.

Defining Users

The days of calling them patrons seem nostalgic, but whether libraries call them users, patrons, clients, or customers, an important shift has taken place in defining a library's user base. Many of these new services offer phase one of the Holy Grail that is linking catalog with content, but they have also dissociated patrons from libraries. For reasons unknown, this wholesale export of responsibility for library users has gone largely unnoticed. Up until the era of personalized access to content, libraries always took responsibility for authenticating and authorizing their users. No library would consider sending a list of names and vital statistics to the publisher of a printed book (for a detailed discussion of privacy concerns, see chapter 7). Why, then, do libraries encourage users to sign up for services to which the library serves as a gateway or subscription aggregator? That more of these companies have not worked out methods for libraries to utilize existing authentication models, such as patron databases or campus directory services, is astounding; that more libraries have not demanded such models is of great concern.

Most library dot-commers like Questia, netLibrary, ebrary, and eLibrary require users to create personal accounts that reside outside of the library. While some users might readily trade personal information for personalization features, there are longer-term issues involved with this client model. The early adopters of netLibrary's e-book content first raised this issue. Since that firm's model tied subscription material to log-in, rather than to point of access or library authentication, user authorization resided outside of the libraries' control mechanisms. This was, however, presented as a feature, since it allowed users to log in directly to netLibrary from any location and always have access to the collections of their home libraries. What netLibrary did not take into account was that these users would not always be associated with their home libraries—students graduate, public library users move. NetLibrary promised that it would seek some alternative that would remove users from its database on a "regular schedule," but since users were not restricted from creating multiple accounts on the system, this method also proved problematic, both technically and from a bibliographic instruction standpoint. Ebrary will likely face similar challenges when it moves from its per-use model to an organizational licensing scheme; a subscription model for libraries does not obviate the need of patrons to establish local accounts for some of the customized ebrary features. Authorizing the use of library materials is a job historically and best provided by libraries; libraries and vendors must work together to integrate library authentication with licensed resources' features and personalization.

LIBRARIES FIGHT BACK AND CATCH UP
Adaptations of Dot-com Solutions

No one can accuse libraries of complete inaction when it comes to applying dot-com solutions to traditional digital services. In fact, libraries were the quickest to jump on several bandwagons, including search engines, book vendor websites, and various virtual reference tools.

Virtual Reference

In one sense, it is too bad that libraries call this relatively new online service "virtual reference," since there is nothing virtual about it; it is *literally* more work, more expertise, and more effort to provide this service. Calling it "virtual" only detracts from those facts. The label also distracts users from the fact that libraries have been providing alternative reference services since the advent of the suggestion box. With gate-counts declining, most libraries have experienced heavy increases in phone, e-mail, and chat reference queries. Most libraries experimenting—or in full production with—online reference services will usually even relate an anecdote of the patron using online reference services within feet of the physical reference desk.

Two of the most popular applications in libraries are 24/7 and Library Systems and Services' (LSSI's) Virtual Reference Desk Software. The latter is actually powered by eGain, the e-commerce CRM solution, and is customized by LSSI for library reference use. The jury may still be out on the use and popularity surrounding online reference service, but early indications show that it is exceedingly popular, especially since, besides books, reference was one of the last remaining library services that still required a trip to the library for real-time service. A body of literature, and several conference opportunities, are already growing up around this new hot library topic. Book-length treatment of the topic began as early as 1998.[9]

On a national scale, the Internet Public Library (http://www.ipl.org/ref) has been offering e-mail reference service for some time. In 2001, the Library of Congress and OCLC announced a nationwide professional effort to provide virtual reference service around the clock (http://www.loc.gov/rr/digiref/). The service is called QuestionPoint and will allow users to manage their reference systems locally (on an individual level or within a consortium or group of libraries). The local components include ask-a and chat functionality, a local knowledge base, and comprehensive reporting and administrative tools.

No longer the only game in town, libraries have risen to the challenge of virtual reference. When commercial attempts begin to fail due to cost, lack of authority, or simple lack of interest, libraries will be there to offer the service quickly, thoroughly, freely, and authoritatively. Answering questions is definitely an area in which librarians are not prepared to abdicate power.

Online Catalogs and Circulation

As mentioned in the previous chapter, perhaps no other dot-com has received more attention from the library community than Amazon.com. Part fear, part shame, this attention has done more for online catalog development in five years than ILS companies did in the previous twenty. Starting with only the *Books in Print* online data set, Amazon built an online bookselling empire that would eventually expand into other markets, including music, video, computer hardware and software, electronics, toys, and health and beauty. The expansion and financial overextension of Amazon need to be set aside for some specialized treatment of the firm's book catalog, at least for the purposes of this book. Comparisons of this catalog with library online catalogs are not only applicable, they could prove fruitful for the library community.

Given a taste of what the Internet has to offer, users expect more from a normal online catalog, and Amazon (and to a lesser extent Barnes and Noble's BN.com) have set the bar extremely high. In a fashion similar to e-book companies marrying catalog and content, Amazon has succeeded in marrying catalog surrogates with added-value content such as book reviews, chapter excerpts, biographical information, and readers' advisories. Amazon has even applied a library feature that most ILS vendors have not added to their software yet—the ability to submit a search based on any or all of a title's Library of Congress Subject Headings. (See figure 3-5.)

Without tremendous effort, libraries could adopt the well-developed features of Amazon's catalog in order to enrich their patrons' online library experience. Features that promote expert or collegial recommendation, or even serendipitous discovery, would vastly expand the landscape of the traditional online catalog. If the advent of Amazon.com and sites like it does nothing more than cause libraries to address the effectiveness of the online catalog in meeting user needs, then that is sufficient. If the fear of backlash in creating catalogs that are more Amazon-like breeds another decade of inaction, then it will do libraries a great disservice. Here is a (slightly edited) short list of features that self-proclaimed "commercial librarian" Gerry McKiernan posted to the WEB4LIB discussion list in August 2000:

- A ranked list of the most heavily borrowed books
- A chronological listing of search results
- An option of displaying books by user rating
- A "patrons who borrowed this book also borrowed . . ." feature
- A "patrons who borrowed titles by author A also borrowed titles by authors X, Y, and Z" feature

Look for similar books by subject:

Browse for books in:
- Subjects > Reference > Publishing & Books > Library Management
- Subjects > Reference > General
- Subjects > Reference > Publishing & Books > Library Science & Guidance

Search for books by subject:
- ☐ Libraries
- ☐ United States
- ☐ Automation
- ☐ Libraries and electronic publi
- ☐ Library Science (General)
- ☐ Library Automation
- ☐ Education / Teaching
- ☐ Language Arts & Disciplines
- ☐ Library & Information Science
- ☐ Information Technology

> Find books matching ALL checked subjects
> i.e., each book must be in subject 1 AND subject 2 AND ...

FIGURE 3-5   In 2001, Amazon.com added the cornerstone of the library MARC record, the Library of Congress Subject Headings. Note that a combined search is possible, a feature that few library system vendors offer themselves. © 2002, courtesy of Amazon.com, Inc. All rights reserved.

- A "look for similar books by subject/browse for books in [full listing of associated subject headings]" feature
- A "search for books by subject" feature with listings of headings and associated check-off boxes[10]

Although slower paced, the Amazon-like library catalog has been coming along, as ILS vendors tackle technical hurdles and librarians tackle philosophical ones. Sirsi's iBistro (also marketed as iLink to academic libraries) was one of the first library automation products to enhance its catalog interface with added-value content. Although libraries have been adding URLs and table of contents data to MARC records for years, iBistro represented a major departure in that it did not add the new content to the MARC database itself. Instead, it licensed data from a company called Syndetic Solutions, which uses its own data-streaming technology to add content to hit list and record displays on-the-fly. Other ILS vendors, notably Innovative Interfaces, have followed suit with similar added-value content. (See figures 3-6 and 3-7.) Innovative stands alone in its effort to add the valuable content in staff modules as well, allowing collection managers or acquisitions staff to view cover art and book reviews before making a purchase, for example.

FIGURE 3-6   Sirsi's iLink catalog record. © 2002, Sirsi Corp. All rights reserved.

Libraries can also continue to add content enrichment in a fashion similar to ebrary's InfoTools, mentioned previously. By passing queries and highlighted text to other web common gateway interfaces (CGIs), libraries can integrate third-party content services without building an all-inclusive database. Think of this as one-trip shopping, as opposed to one-stop shopping. In the accompanying example from the NCSU Libraries (see figure 3-8), the

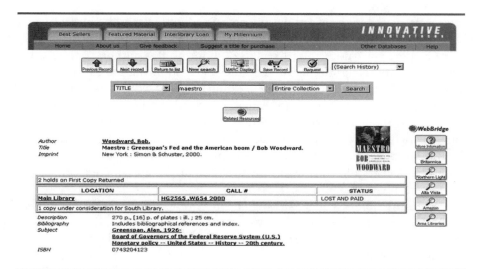

FIGURE 3-7   Innovative Interfaces' Millennium Access Plus catalog enrichment.
© 2002, Innovative Interfaces, Inc. All rights reserved.

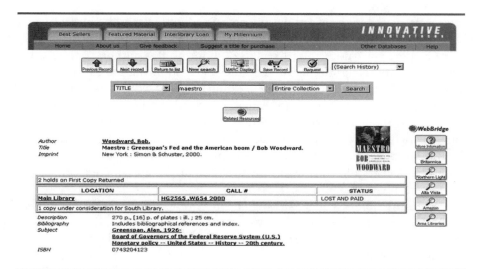

FIGURE 3-8   NCSU Libraries catalog record display. The enriched display is created
without any third-party data or added expense. © 2002, NCSU
Libraries. All rights reserved.

user is presented with several options associated with either the initial catalog search or metadata from the bibliographic record.

Clicking on "more titles like this," "more by this author," or the title's associated subject headings will keep the user within the local catalog, passing the metadata selected to the existing catalog search CGI. Choosing "google search" or "web image search" will send the user to those external resources with elements of the 245 title as the search term (this could be any other part of the record as well, such as subject or author). Serial titles offer an option to "search for electronic versions," which queries an external database of full-text titles that will lead the user to the appropriate copy for a given citation. (See figure 3-9.)

Even the library standard *Books in Print* from R. R. Bowker has revved up to Internet speed to provide a web front-end for its old CD-ROM database, complete with reviews, metadata searches, and enriched content. Other aggregators of the *Books in Print* data, such as InfoTrac, have added similar links. The fate of such *Books in Print* features is unknown, however, since R. R. Bowker's owner, Reed Elsevier, put the company up for sale in 2001.

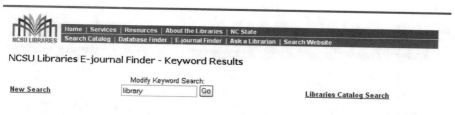

NCSU Libraries E-journal Finder - Keyword Results

New Search   Modify Keyword Search: **Libraries Catalog Search**
                        library   [Go]

Your search for "**library**" found **83** items:

TITLE	AVAILABILITY	START DATE	END DATE	PROVIDER
Academic and Library Computing	Selected Articles	4/1/1991	5/1/1992	InfoTrac OneFile
"African Journal of Library, Archives & Information Science"	Selected Articles	4/1/1998	Present	Wilson OmniFile: Full Text Mega Edition
Australian Library Journal	Selected Articles	2/1/2000	Present	InfoTrac Custom
Australian Library Journal	Selected Articles	2/1/2000	Present	InfoTrac OneFile
Electronic Library	Full Issue	1999	Present	Emerald Fulltext
Georgia Library Quarterly	Selected Articles	3/1/1998	Present	Wilson OmniFile: Full Text Mega Edition
International Information & Library Review	Full Issue	1993	2001	AP Ideal - Academic Press
Journal (California School Library Association)	Selected	0/1/1007	0/1/1007	Wilson OmniFile: Full Text

FIGURE 3-9   NCSU Libraries' E-journal Finder searches for full electronic journal titles or aggregated full-text resources. © 2002, NCSU Libraries. All rights reserved.

It does not take much to make a library's online catalog more useful to patrons, but abandoning tradition by providing links to resources outside of libraries' control or making available third-party editorial data (like book reviews) within the catalog are not easy tasks. Some libraries may conclude that trying to compete with the services offered by sites like Amazon is not worth the effort, but those that do will be creating familiar interfaces with features appreciated by online consumers.

Google the Library

At some undetermined point in web history, Google surpassed AltaVista as the Web's premier search engine. This popularity may be due to the simplicity of its interface, the whimsical curiosity of the "I Feel Lucky" button, or the name that has quickly become noun, verb, and adjective (as in "Go to Google," "Google it," and "Google world"). Google's unique algorithm, based partly on the number of external pages that link to a resource, made its retrieval system highly accurate; and whether or not its popularity wanes when something even newer comes along, the concept of Google is firmly embedded in the culture of the Internet. Two particular features of the Google world are already making their way into the library world of technology.

Metasearching

The supposed Holy Grail of library resource searching (okay, so there are *two* Holy Grails in this chapter), Google's simple interface that searches everything has become one of the latest luxuries for library users. Elements of metasearching, i.e., the ability to submit a search to several similar or disparate databases, have been around for quite some time—Silver Platter, Z39.50 broadcast, and several Internet search engines—but some librarians still dream of the day when a single submit button will retrieve all that they are looking for. ILS vendors, quicker on the uptake than usual, have almost all come up with a proprietary solution for the multiple search option, although most of these interfaces are merely repurposed versions of Z39.50 clients. The desire to solve the complexities of metasearching had simple roots in the (supposed) bibliographic instruction impossibility of explaining to users that they must go to three main locations to find content: the catalog for books, abstract and index databases for journal articles, and journal aggregators for online full text.

In order to combat this problem, vendors and libraries first turned to Z39.50, the protocol which had been supposedly supplanted by web interfaces. Libraries and vendors alike, however, had overlooked the potential of

Z39.50's broadcast search capabilities. Two inherent problems remain: Z39.50 does not scale to the breadth of resources available, and not all database resources support Z39.50 access to their servers; hence the proprietary solutions of products like MetaFind (Innovative Interfaces), MetaLib (Ex Libris), ENCompass (Endeavor), OneSearch (Sirsi), MuseGlobal, and many more. (See figures 3-10 to 3-12.)

Metasearch and retrieval is one of the most interesting areas of library automation to watch right now. Which solution will offer the best results without watering down content, controlled vocabulary, and vendor feature sets? It will likely be some time before this is figured out. In the meantime, libraries are fortunate to be working closely with ILS and library automation vendors to determine exactly how this software will work.

Fuzzy Matching

Library catalogs have a habit of unkindness when it comes to failed searches. By contrast, search engines like Google have a lot more content to work with in order to attempt positive feedback for almost any query. While most library catalogs will likely never have the capabilities of Google, libraries and their

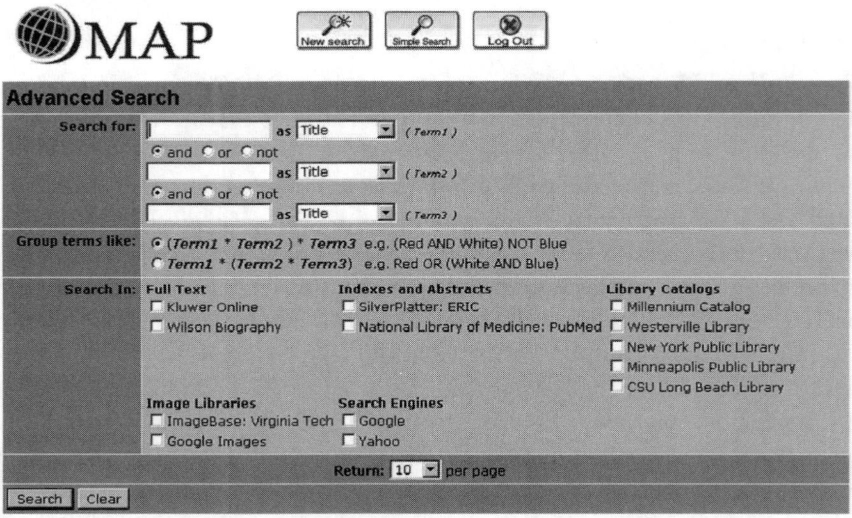

FIGURE 3-10   Innovative Interfaces' MetaFind search engine.

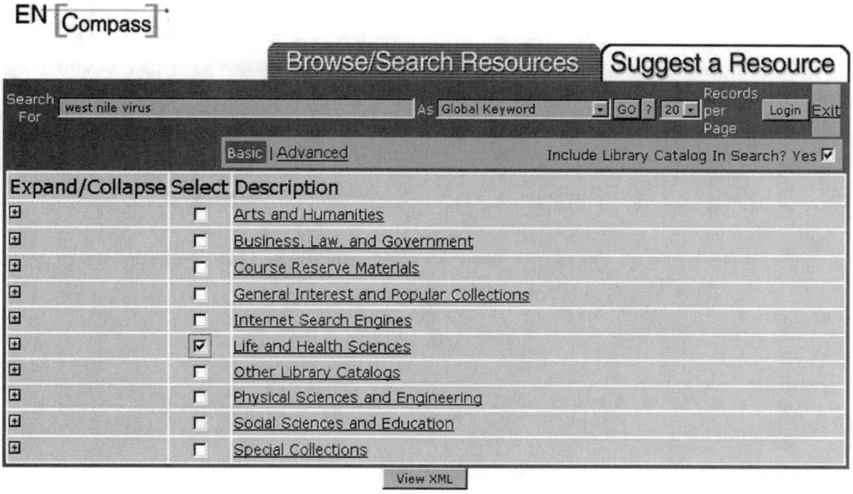

FIGURE 3-11   Endeavor's ENCompass search engine. © 2002, Endeavor Information Systems. All rights reserved.

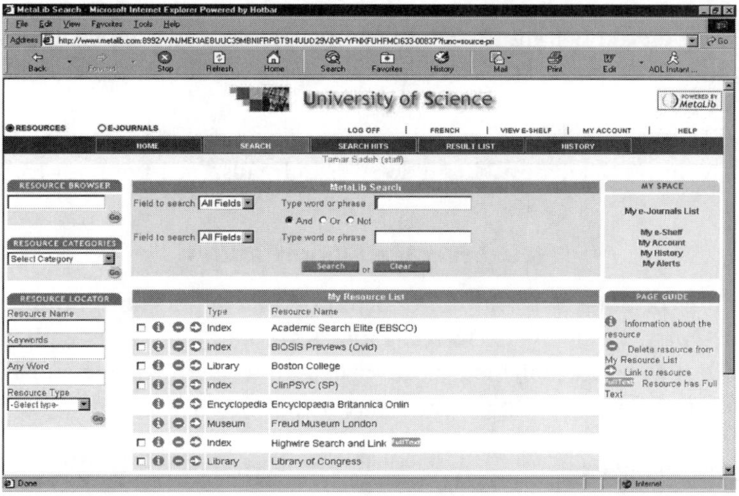

FIGURE 3-12   Ex Libris's MetaLib search engine. © 2002, Ex Libris. All rights reserved.

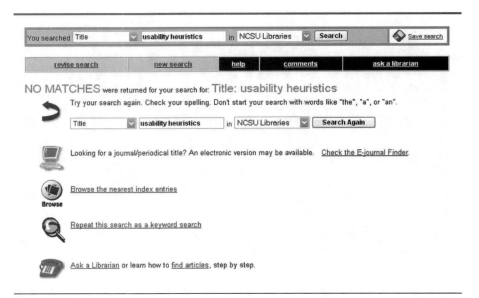

FIGURE 3-13   NCSU Libraries' fuzzy matching. The failed search offers redirections
to various resources, and opportunities to rephrase the query.
© 2002, NCSU Libraries. All rights reserved.

vendors could do much more than flip author names and remove leading articles in order to help users conduct searches. Failed catalog searches could offer
spell-checkers, add synonym lists for words with multiple versions (such as
"theatre" or "catalogue"), expand searches to matching thesauri, or pass
searches to other databases when a local search fails. (See figure 3-13.)

New Leverage Opportunities

The features of dot-coms and their corresponding application in libraries are
not necessarily mutually exclusive. Libraries could do more with various
Internet businesses to enhance their services and raise awareness of libraries
in the information marketplace. Here are a few examples.

Ask Jeeves Redirect

Ask Jeeves could use IP detection to determine the searcher's local public
library and closest academic one. One of the options might be to search that
local catalog for key terms in the query.

Amazon Book Sales

Libraries could use Amazon.com to resell used books. While Amazon takes a large cut from these sales, libraries could maintain an ongoing database of withdrawn and donated titles for sale, rather than relying on annual, labor-intensive book sales.

Amazon Redirect

Libraries might add options to buy the book from Amazon when it is not available locally. A less radical approach to this might be to redirect users to the local independent or campus bookstore. Amazingly, most campus bookstores do not offer a searchable database for their catalog of books.

Google Answers

Google recently announced a new fee-based reference question service.[11] Imagine if the Library of Congress/OCLC service were to join this effort and provide low-cost reference services to the entire world. The traffic would undoubtedly prove overwhelming at first, but the publicity would be impressive.

Dot-commers are the newcomers in the information industry, and librarians should cease being timid, vindictive, and suspicious of their foray into the realm once dominated by their profession. If libraries apply equal effort in building better services, evaluating the services of competitors, and building bridges to vendors and dot-coms, mutually beneficial solutions will present themselves.

Notes

The epigraph for this chapter is from Mick O'Leary, "New Academic Information Model Bypasses Libraries," *Online* 25, no. 4 (2001): 72.

1. Questia website, at http://www.questia.com/aboutQuestia/faqLibrary.html#faq2. One can hardly help but editorialize at the backhanded compliment that gives libraries a "key role" in the future of research.
2. Susan Gibbons, "Growing Competition for Libraries," *Library Hi Tech* 19, no. 4 (2001): 363.
3. Gibbons, "Growing Competition," 363–64
4. Ibid., 366.
5. Mick O'Leary, "Ebrary Shapes New Ebook Paradigm," *EContent* 24, no. 2 (2001): 58.

6. Susan Gibbons, "Interview with Christopher Warnock, CEO, CTO and Co-Founder of ebrary," *Librarian's eBook Newsletter* 2, no. 4 (2002).

7. Susan Gibbons, "Long-Awaited ebrary Has Arrived," *Librarian's eBook Newsletter* 2, no. 3 (2002).

8. O'Leary, "Ebrary Shapes," 58.

9. See 2nd Digital Reference Conference (Seattle, Wash., 2000), *Facets of Digital Reference* (Syracuse: ERIC Clearing House, 2001); Anne G. Lipow, *Virtual Reference Desk Training Manual* (El Dorado Hills, Calif.: Library Solutions, 2001); R. David Lanks and Abby S. Kasowitz, *The AskA Starter Kit: How to Build and Maintain Digital Reference Services* (Syracuse: ERIC Clearing House, 1998).

10. Gerry McKiernan, e-mail [WEB4LIB], August 2000.

11. See https://answers.google.com/answers/main. This is another good example of a dot-com creating better branding than libraries. "Ask a Librarian" services and the Library of Congress's QuestionPoint both give prominence to *asking* questions, while Google puts the emphasis where it should be, on *answers.*

4 | BUSINESS MODELS FOR DIGITAL LIBRARY SERVICES

Only recently has discussing the "business of libraries" become possible without the usual abhorrent reaction from librarians who view business and libraries as so diametrically opposed as to be enemies. To apply business rules to the heart of academia or to the free public library would be like stripping the very culture of libraries, attacking their mission, and commodifying information. But suddenly, information has become a commodity, and businesses—much to the library profession's chagrin—are modeling information services and challenging the (still nearly unnoticed) foe.

Since one of the major themes of this book is how libraries can learn from their private sector counterparts, it makes perfect sense to investigate the methods that companies use to determine the viability of a new product or service. Traditionally, libraries have set themselves apart from businesses, summarily dismissing the processes that are required to run a successful enterprise. Given the challenges and competition now presented by business, however, applying business's successful practices, while leveraging the strategic advantage that libraries have in their more altruistic nature, will leave libraries poised to succeed where many information businesses are doomed to fail. Running services smoothly and keeping products and services relevant to the organizational mission not only makes good libraries, it makes good business sense.

THE BUSINESS OF LIBRARIES

Eric Ormsby, formerly of Princeton University Library, points to the 1970s as the decade when most research library directors were forced to seek budgetary relief in an economic climate more and more hostile to universities in general, and libraries in particular. Ormsby approaches the new business thinking in libraries with disdain:

> [L]ibrary directors accustomed to submitting elegantly drafted and wryly understated annual reports, were now being asked to draw up "business plans" for their operations. Efficiency experts, systems analysts, and high-priced consultants were not far behind. In all this, perhaps the greatest harm occurred because the research library was simplistically likened to any other large and complex organization when in fact its distinctive operations, requirements, and, yes, institutional culture—in short, all those factors that had made our great libraries great—were utterly at variance with those of a factory or a corporation.[1]

While Ormsby's piece on the battle of print *versus* digital is inspiring, whimsical, and ultimately poignant, his distaste for library business models should remain within its historical context. Yes, focusing on the bottom line in the 1970s (and most of the two decades that followed) caused irreparable harm to libraries, mostly to their collections. But how one focuses on the bottom line can go a long way to create a silver lining around an otherwise darker and darker cloud. Ironically, automation boomed in an era when print collections dwindled, and Ormsby adequately ridicules the "smokescreen panacea of 'networking.'"[2] Nevertheless—and without trying to frame this as a means that justifies the end—automation's boom has meant the unprecedented growth of new library services for an expanding and increasingly diverse patron base faced, since the advent of the Internet, with a seemingly geometric increase in the number and variety of information resources available from month to month. Moreover, Internet business models—both those that libraries would consider in the library automation industry and those from outside of it—have challenged libraries to step up to the plate in an era where resources that are good and free are in danger of being supplanted by those that are fast and cheap. With a user populace malnourished despite a glut of available information, libraries have sought every opportunity to capitalize on networked solutions, resource sharing, and digital solutions that will make library functions more efficient and the experience of the user more fruitful.

In this light, the bottom line takes on new meaning. In an Internet age where only the fittest services survive, business service models make more sense. Respect is bestowed upon Internet sites and services that users appreciate; if libraries take those sites and services to heart, then the respect will follow. Now that naive notions of binary digits replacing ink on paper anytime in the near future are dwindling, libraries have within their grasp the ability to make the most of automated services, while preserving their traditional roles as gathering places, cultural centers, and egalitarian sources of information and knowledge.

DIGITAL SERVICE
Businesslike Revaluation

One myth worth disposing of at the outset is the adolescent notion that digital libraries will exist as ancillary services provided by the traditional library. The digital library—a comprehensive definition will not be attempted here—encompasses not only collections in digital form, but digital *services* that continue to define the library as a place. The digital–traditional relationship is symbiotic, not parasitic; digital tools, services, and expertise exist to enhance the services and collections of libraries, not necessarily to replace them. To that end, libraries, whether they realize it or not, make decisions about digital services and automation solutions in a manner consistent with the mission of building and describing traditional collections. That the methods vary—or are completely nonexistent—when compared to their print counterparts, however, is cause for concern.

There is a distinction that needs to be made here between building digital libraries—the suite of automated services and online collections that complement print resources—and digitization, the factorylike conversion to or creation of digital content. The "digital" focus in this book is more on services than digitized collections, which require separate treatment; in fact, digitization has been the focal point of the digital library for so long that digital services—both homegrown and purchased through vendors—have lacked the attention they deserve given their reach. As libraries enter what might be described as the second generation of the digital library, one focused on service as much as collections, much of the first generation of services that paralleled the building of digital collections requires reevaluation, repurposing, revamping, or even reduction. Returning to the much-maligned library business model, libraries could, at the very least, begin to take a product development and product management approach to digital services and collections.

The major problem with a formal approach to addressing digital library services is that most library services on the Web began as grassroots efforts. With what began as a guarded embrace of web technology in the early 1990s, libraries cautiously mounted home pages with links to library hours, directions, circulation policies, and—even more cautiously—a telnet link to the online catalog. By the mid- to late 1990s, library web services resembled what Alison Head refers to as "crazy quilts of whimsical design, patches of disjointed content, and jumbles of color."[3] Eavesdrop on most library website redesign meetings in the twenty-first century and you will most likely encounter a fierce debate on the distinctions between "collections" and "services," between "reference and instruction" and "ask a librarian," between "databases" and "indexes and abstracts." The debate proves nearly futile as libraries try to fit several centuries of collections, services, and traditions onto an easy-to-use, navigable, and efficient website.

Nevertheless, a measured approach to designing digital library services could benefit most libraries. The first goal is making the right choices regarding projects that the library takes on; secondly, taking the *project* into the *product* phase will either justify the effort expended, or condemn the service to several months or years of disuse, misuse, or at best misunderstanding. This chapter, however, is not intended to quote chapter and verse on project management; rather, it is meant to place the focus on the project at the stage of conception, and then to refocus attention on post-project support for new services, i.e., so-called product management. This approach, traditionally applied in businesses, is completely applicable to library practice, and can only serve to strengthen a suite of established services by sound measures taken to sustain existing library products and create new ones.

ORDER TO CHAOS
Applying Business Rules in Libraries

Libraries, especially academic ones, excel at projects. It is one of the characteristics that distinguishes them from the bottom-line, bottom-dollar mentality under which most businesses either prosper or suffer. And librarians take pride in the altruistic nature of their work; toil, even if for the benefit of just one reader (so says Ranganathan, no?), is worth the effort. In reality, however, the virtual representation of library services must, by design, have an equalizing effect, reaching the largest possible audience with the least amount of effort. Unfortunately, though, few libraries seem to have a structured approach to designing new services. The rest of this chapter will seek to establish a broad outline of business model planning for library services, and explore the opportunities of shared development in a profession poised to take advantage of the networked environment of information.

Business Model Planning

Taking advantage of examples close to home, the Libraries at North Carolina State University recognized in the late 1990s that the creation of new services was quickly outpacing the libraries' existing infrastructure for approving, developing, and supporting those new services, which seemed universally to contain a digital component. Thanks to a long collections relationship, the Libraries already had strong ties with the university's College of Management. In the spring 2000 semester, two faculty members in the Business Management Department, Lynda Aiman-Smith and Mitzi Montoya-Weiss, presented broad instructions for applying business models to library services.[4] Based on their experience in training undergraduates and graduate students to work and lead in the private sector, Aiman-Smith and Montoya-Weiss proposed the unorthodox approach of using business processes to address library service needs. This is the sort of approach that most library vendors and dot-com entrepreneurs would need to take in order to make a successful bid for venture capital or to convince customers of the practicality of a new service. It makes sense to apply these same rules in libraries. An expanded outline based on Aiman-Smith and Montoya-Weiss's recommended procedure follows.

Stage One: Preliminary Analysis

An unattributed maxim in the world of information technology goes like this: solve only *known* problems. In the grassroots culture of library automation development described above, this important maxim sometimes fades from view. Lack of long-range planning easily clouds the work of committees, administrators, and, most often, individuals with the time and autonomy to dream up new services. Simply knowing what problem is being solved—through preliminary analysis—can refocus a library's attention on its primary mission.

The preliminary analysis of new digital services, whether performed by an individual or vetted by a formal committee, should make a careful assessment of four major areas.

1. *Articulate expected benefits.* These benefits can be broken down into customer value, competitive value, and political value. The three are not mutually exclusive, nor are all three necessary to realize an overall benefit. Moreover, this step alone propels the business model plan beyond the "solve known problems" hurdle.

2. *Estimate costs.* Costs should not be limited, as they often are in digital services projects, to initial hardware and software expenditures, or to fixed costs that might be articulated in a grant proposal. Costs should include development, delivery, and maintenance of the service. Moreover, the analysis should include what are traditionally thought of as sunk costs as well. Taking the corporate software business as an example, writing new software code represents a major sunk cost; this generalization assumes that existing staff will perform the requisite tasks and that licensing of third-party products is not required for the project. As such, any new project plan includes the estimation of "programmer hours" required to complete the task. Similarly, libraries need to estimate the cost in staff time, web development requirements, and the cost of outside professional services such as data entry, programming, interface design, and temporary staffing needs. This cost assessment will likely take a library through the development and delivery phases; maintenance of the resulting product, however, should not be overlooked. Given the pace of today's technology, newly released products are almost always a heartbeat away from becoming legacy products. This fact requires a realistic assessment of the ongoing maintenance costs associated with a new library service.

3. *Risk assessment.* A careful assessment of the costs associated with launching a new service will allow a library to apply a corresponding opportunity cost for the proposed service. For example, if a library plans to switch from paper delivery of overdue and pickup notices to online delivery of notices, the cost of automating the process should be compared to the cost of keeping the current system, that is, if saving money on the transaction is one of the delineated benefits. Moreover, the cost should also be compared to the cost of developing a completely different project, given the opportunity. In either case, if the opportunity cost is too high for deploying the new service, an alternative approach might be needed. Another factor in risk assessment has to do with measuring the cost of the success or failure of the service. If the cost benefit of success is great, then the risk of the investment is worth the effort; if the cost of failure—including political and competitive costs—is even greater than the financial cost of implementing a new service, the library should give careful thought to the risk.

4. *Timing.* The time needed to develop a new service goes hand in hand with the timing of the release of that new service. Any new service proposal should include a rough timeline based on an analysis of the time needed to complete the project. The time-sensitive nature of some projects (for example, acquiring the necessary disk space for an impending requirement from the graduate school to submit electronic theses to the library) might confine the library to certain windows of opportunity to deploy a new service; other

projects might be tied to fiscal or calendar year cycles, elections of new library boards, or the end of a college semester. All of these attributes should be included in the preliminary analysis.

At this stage of the proposal, all the analysis is internal to the library. The main objectives of the analysis are to evaluate the service concepts critically and relative to existing services or new service alternatives. It might be helpful to establish a list of heuristics ("rules of thumb") to aid in the objective evaluation of new concepts. Moreover, the analysis process should include soliciting the multiple and diverse perspectives of all major stakeholders in the library service implementation.

Stage Two: Investigation and Validation

One might think of stage one as the conceptual description that allows the proponents of a new service to begin stage two with the political, strategic, and administrative blessing of the library organization. In business and libraries (arguably more so in libraries), it is amazing how good ideas can often fail to reach fruition simply because certain stakeholders did not feel they played an adequate role in the decision. It is equally amazing how effectively an administrative mandate (even a rubber stamp) can counter those ill feelings. Much of stage two will be continued validation of stage one, with a few added pieces of the investigation.

Once proponents have estimated the costs, benefits, and time needed to complete a project, they must begin to validate all three. This may involve more detailed project management planning—for example, with the use of project software—or simply getting input from more staff to establish realistic expectations for completion. At this point, the service proponents should begin to solicit feedback from external stakeholders, i.e., patrons. Proponents might accomplish this with focus groups, informal interviews, or more formal elements of usability engineering.[5] The goals in attaining user feedback are to validate the assumptions made about the necessity of the new business model, more accurately gauge user demand for a new service, and take the first step in identifying missing elements in the design concepts of a new service.

This stage also requires the refinement of cost metrics, i.e., more exact figures regarding the cost to the library that will, in turn, establish the value to the patron. The cost metric itself is up to the library; whether the metric includes every working minute and material cost does not matter, as long as the metric is applied consistently, not only for a single project, but across several projects when they are being compared with one another. This is usually where libraries begin to have a problem. Determining costs, however, should not be anathema to a profession focused on maintaining stability in an information economy that seemingly threatens the traditional library model. A quick look at service *value,* in the context of cost, might help.

The Value Balance Equation

- benefit (importance to the patron) − cost (to the patron) = customer value
- benefit (importance to the library) − cost (to provide) = value delivery[6]

The challenge in the value balance equation comes in relating customer value to library value. Frankly, this represents one area where business and libraries clash, with the advantage going to the latter. A business might decide that a high customer value and a low value delivery present an incompatible business model; a library might want to take a more careful look at the value delivery component, but it can still decide to provide the service at a loss to its bottom line. When such a service maintains a high customer value—primarily due to the low cost to the patron, which is subsidized by the library—the library will be viewed as providing service that has no commercial equivalent. In an age where Internet service is more and more driven by commercial interest, these sorts of advantages will play a key role in the success of libraries. Moreover, looking at the two equation results—customer value and value delivery—together is important because it can expose artificial inflation of customer value that is based solely on a library bearing the costs. Higher costs, generally, should go hand in hand with a high level of importance to the library, but this does not necessarily mean that libraries should bear the cost of every service that has a high benefit to the customer. Take printing and photocopying, for example—most libraries provide some sort of printing service. The benefit to the patron is quite high; no one wants to write out by hand what can easily be printed or copied. Arriving at a reasonable cost-recovery charge for such a service can continue to maintain a high customer value, while minimizing the cost to the library. Several academic libraries continue to provide free services that patrons would gladly pay nominal amounts to obtain, since the value to them remains high. Better determination of those values might even require the assistance of business experts.

The library may determine that a new service requires more formal market research. Libraries tend to do market research in a reactive mode that seeks to prove the existence of a service is worth its maintenance. More importantly, libraries should strive to determine market relevance *before* a service is offered. But before going out and hiring an expensive marketing firm to establish that patrons appreciate library services, proponents might want to leverage the research that is already being done by corporate entities trying to capture a share of the library market. Libraries should not only perform literature reviews that trap them in a circular rut of keeping up with the Joneses; literature outside the library domain will reveal market research that libraries can use to their advantage in determining the next wave of service. The only remaining challenge, then, is distinguishing between a sustainable trend and a fad.

Stage Three: Development

More in-depth market analysis continues into stage three, as proponents of the new service begin the detailed work of writing the technical specifications that will define that service. Keep in mind that the focus is on digital services for the purpose of this discussion. Any software company, whether it is releasing a new product or enhancing an old one, starts its development with specifications. The assumption here—and one that would benefit libraries as well—is that anyone can implement the specifications that are written. In many library environments, the main proponent might be the same person actually coding the software, web page, or digital service; this should not exempt that individual from documenting a technical specification. This way, no matter what happens in the future, there is a record of how the development stage progressed. In other cases, the library might not have the requisite expertise among its own personnel, but might have the financial support to develop a new service. In this scenario, the library might contract with programming expertise that has no contextual grounding in a library business model. This makes careful and detailed specifications for the service all the more important. How to actually write a technical specification is beyond the scope of this book, but several models can be found in both library and computer science literature; this is even an area where libraries could learn a great deal from their vendor counterparts. (See chapter 5.)

At this stage, the library should begin to address workflow issues and staff competencies. Take a library laptop-lending service as an example. When determining where to place the service, the existing workflow of the reserves desk, for example, is called into question. The service will be launched at the beginning of the semester, the busiest time for the reserves staff, which is still processing faculty reserves. Moreover, over the years, some staff may have sought assignments at the reserves desk in order to escape the rapidly escalating dependence on automation; the separate paper functions of reserves represented a quiet refuge. Would these staff members be able to handle even the simplest question about using the attached floppy drive that comes with the laptop? With regard to both workflow and competency issues, the workflow process might be better handled, in this fictitious example, at the main circulation desk, where the beginning of the semester is quieter, and the technical competencies higher. This careful analysis will have a ripple effect for the entire project.

As more internal stakeholders bring their expertise to the project, other development requirements will come to light. Technical issues should be addressed early on, in relation to the established specifications for the service. These requirements can often be the most expensive, even if they're not the most difficult ones. Moreover, some services might expose legal liabilities that were not perceived in the original business plan. For example, a digitization project might raise access issues and copyright concerns. Hurdles like these can often seem much higher than their technical counterparts. To give another example, technically it is simple to place a thumbnail image of a digitized image on a database hit list; whether doing so is legal or not is a different matter altogether. Compliance with the Americans with Disabilities Act (ADA), especially for digital services with no print or analog equivalent, can also raise concerns. Libraries should prepare themselves for possible legal ramifications when providing access to diverse communities. Finally, professional and ethical concerns are especially important in the library profession. ADA compliance is an ethical concern, as well as a legal one. Protecting privacy, providing fair and equitable access, and ensuring service goals that meet libraries' high quality standards represent just a few examples of development obstacles that early and careful analysis can combat.

By the end of the development stage, the library should have a detailed workflow, an analysis of all technical and financial requirements, and a business plan that will ensure the proper implementation of the new service. And by now, the urge to implement will also be great.

Stage Four: Prototype and Pilot

Stage four is when many businesses and libraries mistakenly perform market research. Two important lessons to keep in mind during the prototype stage are that market acceptance should not be determined during a pilot; and beta testing should not be a primary usability tool. This does not mean that neither can contribute to a successful implementation; rather, they should only serve to validate the previous three business model stages. Prototyping lends validation, assures service quality, gauges staff and patron reaction, serves to gather qualitative and quantitative data, and helps determine whether a business plan should be rolled out or rescaled.

Stage Five: Implementation and Follow-Up

Implementation is simple compared to follow-up. If the first four stages have been carefully executed throughout the process, then organizational readiness should not represent a major hurdle. Nevertheless, ensuring that staff are prepared will smooth any service transitions. The library should have already been thinking about marketing approaches by now, but this is the stage at which the library implements those strategies. In promotional planning, the tool should match the service objectives and the allocated budget. For example, mass mailing to announce a service to a niche community might not make sense; conversely, a simple sign in the physical building announcing the availability of resources from remote locations also seems illogical.

The library, like a business, has several promotional tools at its disposal: public relations, personal selling, direct mail, push technology (e-mail), advertising, and simple word of mouth. (See figure 4-1.)

Advertising
Reaches Many Customers
Expensive
Impersonal

Personal Selling
Personal Interaction
Expensive
Builds Relationships

Sales Promotion
Provides Strong Incentives to Try
Short-Lived

Public Relations
Believable, Effective
Economical
Impersonal and Underused

Direct Marketing
Nonpublic, Immediate, Customized
Labor-Intensive
Interactive

FIGURE 4-1 Promotional toolchart. From Lynda Aiman-Smith and Mitzi Montoya-Weiss, "Application of Business Models to the Library: Service Portfolio Mapping."

Which tool the library uses might not even prove as vital as the timing of such promotions. The timing should be concentrated, continuous, or intermittent. Generally, libraries depend on the first of these and ignore the last two. Even worse, the existence of a web page or archived press release is considered continuous advertising. This is like a business relying on an old magazine issue to convey its current advertising needs. While continuous promotion might cause budgetary problems, it is more likely a problem for an organization that has a focus on multiple independent services; a library cannot rest on the laurels of one new product in order to continually draw customers. An intermittent promotional strategy, however, might prove more fruitful. Whether academic, public, or special, all libraries contend with shifting, rolling, and migratory user populations. If the benefit of a service does not decrease over time, but the population changes, libraries must develop strategies to promote existing services. Failure to do so results in a self-fulfilled prophecy of legacy services. A simple rule of thumb might be to promote a new service—either continuously or intermittently—for as long as it took to reach the final stage of the business model process. At the end of that promotional cycle, the library might reevaluate the value balance equation to determine the best interval for continued service promotion.

Unfortunately, the work does not end here. Post-implementation attention to new services continues for the life of the product. This distinction between projects and products is important because how a library treats a completed project (now a product) is as important as the selection of the next project that the library will undertake. Simply moving on to the next project does a disservice to the hard work that has gone into earlier ones. Feedback from key stakeholders will continue, and the library must establish a practice of product management that equals the effort and benefit established during the business model planning. This iterative approach to services will keep libraries busy as they add more and more services, and will inform future business model planning activities.

The business model analysis presented above is designed to inform management decisions regarding the ultimate implementation and ongoing product management of library services. While the foregoing examples, and those at the end of this chapter, focus on digital services, there is no need for the library to limit itself in this way; it is done here simply because almost every new service idea these days has a large digital component. As Carolyn Argentati, associate director for public services, noted in her summary of the NCSU Libraries' Business Model Planning workshop:

[The business model approach] ensures that these ideas are documented with clear and objective data and that their implications are well understood, not only by staff members or teams most directly involved ("champions") but also by other departments/divisions, library management, administration, and ultimately by library users and the campus community.[7]

NCSU Libraries adopted the business model planning process in 2001–02. Most of the working participants agree that a consistent implementation over time has tremendous potential to save time, facilitate efficient use of limited resources, and enhance the recognition of the libraries as a leading service provider, both locally and internationally.

KEEPING PRODUCTS AND SERVICES RELEVANT

As was mentioned earlier, as soon as one service is "in the can," it already needs more attention to sustain it. With so many projects on the horizon, however, it proves difficult to maintain objective focus on a project that is viewed as complete. Moreover, the key proponents might already be weary of the service itself, especially after such a long, formal process, or they may be so wrapped up in it that they cannot let go. Despite this, libraries should be aware of three traps into which they can fall after a service has been released: smothering, orphaning, or neglect.

Product Smothering

Sometimes so much effort can go into the development and release of a new service or product that it begins to take on a life of its own; the whole becomes disproportionately greater than the sum of its parts. This is especially true for a staff member who becomes so closely involved with the management of a product that all other work pales—and suffers—by comparison. This is not to say that smothering is always bad; it can serve as an indicator that the product or service requires full-time attention by a dedicated portion of staff resources. This is, after all, how most systems librarians, especially librarians dedicated to the integrated library system, came into existence. But when the return on the investment of time and attention begins to diminish, library administrators, or other objective parties, should step in, not only for the sake of the service, but also for the sake of the staff who dedicate their time to it.

Examples abound in nearly every library. A library portal (personalized access to library resources) might, in theory, alleviate the information overload from which users suffer. It might even work, in practice, to reduce such overload for the early adopters that create a personal account for the "MyLibrary" service. When tremendous resources, however, are dedicated to a service that has few users, reason and boundaries must take over. Digitization projects can also come to define a library's digital existence. The completion of a major project, the benchmarking of certain grant-funded goals, or the consuming nature of dedicated hard work might take a product well beyond the scope of its original business model planning.

Smothering might also involve a service or product to which an inappropriate number of disparate staff are dedicating their time. In large organizations, it is easy for several people to be working in different ways to create or improve the same service. At its worst, this becomes solutions looking for problems. One management approach might support the notion that competition breeds innovation, but in organizations with limited resources, putting these people on the same team means a more efficient approach to serving users. With the business model—either new or historic—in hand, determining the proper level of staff resources is an easier task for the library.

Product Orphaning

The opposite of product smothering is product orphaning. While it is possible that too much time devoted to the development of a new service might make it difficult for staff to move on to something new, it's equally possible that such a singular focus can make development staff long to get as far away as possible from a service once it is in production. Though key developers might be the most logical choice for product managers, they do not always have to serve in both roles; they do, however, need to serve as primary proponents for further nurturing and support for the newly released service. If the service is not worthy of such attention so close to its initial release, then the library should probably rethink its long-term impact and sustainability.

Other orphaned products are justly left so, and, without a service owner or dedicated service base, should be considered for digital weeding. Businesses have a distinct advantage over libraries in this area. Since economic feasibility can determine the future (or lack thereof) of a service, business interests have an easier time weeding or deprecating services from their suite of offerings. Libraries, on the other hand, have a habit of sustaining a service until the very last user has abandoned it, even if that user is on the library staff. Telnet catalog interfaces are one example, sustained, generally speaking, not because the new web interface is too difficult to use or because it lacks too many features, but because the user investment in the legacy interface is too great. Put another way, it is not that the new interface is too hard to learn, it is that the old interface is too hard to unlearn. The patchwork quilt of library services is filled with tattered and underused squares that deserve stitching, replacement, or even removal.

On the other hand, the mere existence of a product orphan might inspire another staff member to take up responsibility for the service, assuming that the developers of the service have adequately described what care and maintenance of it will entail, and that the library is in favor of such an "adoption" procedure. Such a handoff also proves useful when there is staff turnover among the original project or product management staff. The unanticipated nature of some product orphanings also points to the importance of careful documentation, both in the developmental and support stages. Documentation can keep services, which have been given to new staff, from falling into the final trap of product neglect.

Product Neglect

Situated somewhere between smothering and orphaning, product neglect can either be willful or benign. Examples of both will serve to illustrate these labels. Arrogance, either individual or institutional, constitutes an example of willful neglect. A librarian may decide that he or she knows best which features will benefit users, despite anecdotal or statistical evidence to the contrary. For example, mistaken principles may keep an electronic resources librarian from placing *Ergonomics Abstracts* on the list of electronic databases because, in her mind, its existence as a print serial requires that it be considered an electronic journal, despite the fact that users think of it as an index and abstract *database*. Self-service borrower record access is another example. Since this service is usually provided as part of the online catalog software provided by ILS companies, links to accessing borrower record information are usually tied to the online catalog interface. While this might make sense to an ILS vendor who has no control over services on the library's main website, it makes little sense to the average library patron who does not necessarily couple searching for a book with finding information about his account. Simply placing a link to the borrower record function in a more logical or visible place on the library's website removes the feature from a state of neglect.

Benign neglect is somehow more troubling than its willful counterpart. A perfect example is the online catalog. Initial excitement over the features offered in an online environment—mainly keyword searching—created quite a stir in both the cataloging and public service sections of libraries. For reasons yet to be determined, this supposed panacea of catalog access was enough to sustain the automation desires of most libraries for the next two decades of library automation development. This is not to say that development did not continue on some level; libraries were the lucky recipients of a potpourri of online catalog features, usually based on the whimsical development priorities of the ILS vendors, or the programmers in charge of locally supported systems.

It was not until the advent of the Web and the subsequent success of Internet business models like Amazon, BN.com, and several popular search engines that libraries began to pay attention to the features that seem now to be so obviously missing from the library's online catalog. A small but vocal contingent of librarians simultaneously began to decry the impending death of the online catalog; its path to obscurity was seemingly clear. But if it is true that the catalog is dead, then it's also true that libraries killed it, slowly, with benign neglect. As noted in chapter 2, the fact that companies like Amazon and BN.com could make more of a simple *Books in Print* database in short order simply means that the bar has been raised. But was it raised unfairly? Some in the field might point to the corporate sector's huge influx of capital as too great a challenge for the less than agile nature of library development. But any amount of venture capital should have been no match for over twenty years of intellectual capital. Bemoaning the death of a library's most valuable resource is not a fitting end for the decades of brilliance and hard work that went into its creation.

Some of the neglected features that nonlibrary search services were much quicker to pick up on include relevance ranking of search results, tying user circulation (purchases) to other circulation activity (like Amazon's "users who bought this title also bought . . ."), links to enriched data (book reviews, jacket covers, author biographies, and chapter excerpts), and personalized services and push technology (recommendations, alert services, and readers' advisories).

REDEFINING CULTURE

The most difficult part of all this to swallow, and the part that may have made some librarians skip this chapter or put the book down altogether, is the immediate knee-jerk reaction that a traditionally altruistic profession exhibits when faced with competition from an adversary who seems to be singularly focused on the next fiscal quarter and the bottom line. But in today's Internet age, to think about library services without thinking about business service is to bury one's head in the sand. Despite strong desires to paint them so, libraries are not "utterly at variance" with business, as the quote at the beginning of this chapter suggested. Moreover, there is nothing wrong with watching business from fiscal quarter to fiscal quarter, and emulating its practices, while collectively keeping an eye on the next quarter century and beyond; doing so will not only ensure the future of the library, it will ensure the distinction between businesses and libraries that the latter hold so dear.

Notes

1. Eric Ormsby, "The Battle of the Book: The Research Library Today," *New Criterion* (2001): 13.
2. Ormsby, "Battle of the Book," 11.
3. Alison Head, "Web Redemption and the Promise of Usability," *Online* 23, no. 6 (1999): 21.
4. Lynda Aiman-Smith and Mitzi Montoya-Weiss, "Application of Business Models to the Library: Service Portfolio Mapping" (Raleigh, N.C., 2000). Carolyn Argentati of the NCSU Libraries condensed this presentation into a draft outline for implementation. The partnership between faculty and libraries deserves separate treatment, but is highlighted here for the benefit of comparing business practices to library practices. The relationship is not so rare as to be "strange bedfellows," but a review of the literature shows that it is less common than one might think. Since the faculty is a main constituency of the academic library, partnerships between librarians and the faculty they serve can prove very fruitful.
5. For a more detailed approach to library website usability, see this author's treatise on library web services: Andrew K. Pace, "Optimizing Library Web Services: A Usability Approach," *Library Technology Reports* 38, no. 2 (2002): 1–81.
6. Aiman-Smith and Montoya-Weiss, "Application of Business Models."
7. Carolyn Argentati, "Guidelines for Business Model Planning for Library Services" (Raleigh: North Carolina State University Libraries, Draft Report, 2000).

5 | SHEEP IN WOLVES' CLOTHING

Working inside and
outside the Library

*I don't really call myself a librarian, but I do refer
to myself as being in the field of library science.*
—Joel Summerlin of Corbis, Inc.

I always call myself a librarian. I take a lot of pride in that.
—Linda Feist, information specialist
for Minnesota governor Jesse Ventura

Whether one calls oneself a librarian or merely works in the field of library and information science, the marketplace has certainly shifted a great deal in the past decade. The evolving role of vendors and the rise of the dot-com economy have greatly influenced the way librarians—especially new graduates—make career choices. Unfortunately, the profession does not always adequately acknowledge these shifts. Nontraditional jobs in libraries— for example, information architect or LAN administrator—are viewed as the logical expansion of the profession into areas that benefit from a librarian's expertise. When trained librarians take these sorts of jobs outside of traditional libraries, however, it is often perceived as losing a professional to the private sector. Moreover, hard-line distinctions still remain between master of library science (M.L.S.) degree and computer science professionals, and between M.L.S. holders and paraprofessionals. The former distinction makes little sense given the high level of expertise among nonlibrarian IT staff; the latter relationship is not well leveraged in order to make more professionals out of those with one foot already in the door of the profession.

Whether guided by pride or by acknowledgment that a rose by any other name smells the same outside of a library setting, librarians continue to take work outside of traditional settings, not in droves, but in small trickles of corporate crossover. Arguably, it is library science skills and not technical skills that make library candidates attractive to dot-coms and library vendors; otherwise, technical skill would obviate the need for a library degree. But what exactly makes librarians such attractive candidates for placement outside of libraries? Does an information degree carry extra weight in an information economy? Are librarians capitalizing on the chic of geek? Whatever the reasons, librarians are going to work in several capacities outside of the traditional "academic, public, or special" options into which most librarians fall. Are these different kinds of librarians or different kinds of professions, or both?

The 2001 "Placements & Salaries" report in *Library Journal* reported, rather consistently, that there are plenty of librarian jobs but salaries are flat.[1] Most notable for the purposes of this book is the easily distinguishable difference from the preceding year's survey, proving that the Internet is indeed not immune from the laws of economics. Job placements in the "Other" category fell from 52 in 1999 to 24 in 2000, due in part to limited responses to the survey, but indicative of the downward trend of employment in the dot-com arena. As near as one can tell from the survey, "Other" is meant to encompass all nonlibrary jobs, but does not include the vendor category. Vendor placements, on the other hand, not only offered salary increases of 14 percent over 1999, but also reported a 36 percent increase in library and information science (LIS) placements.

LIBRARY WORK VS. WORK IN LIBRARIES

Love of change and acceptance of uncertainty are just two of the traits that might drive a future librarian to consider work outside of libraries. A frustratingly bureaucratic process and lower pay are just two of the factors that discourage future librarians from pursuing traditional roles in libraries. But whether a librarian embraces the former or tolerates the latter, the entire profession recognizes that working inside and outside libraries entails two different sets of career skills. When it comes to working for a library vendor or a dot-com, however, one might argue that the overlap of skills begins to broaden. Why then do library schools still concentrate on traditional placements? The *Library Journal* report itself equates library *service* with work *in* libraries, noting that out of 1,234 graduates in the year 2000, 1,210, or 98.1 percent, were "employed in some library capacity." Atypically, this total actually includes the 30 job placements among "Vendors." The next paragraph in the survey, however, continues, "of those 1,210 graduates employed *in libraries* . . ."[2] The wording and the format of the statistics make two assumptions that are invalid: first, not working for or in a library should not imply that graduates are not working in some sort of "library capacity"; second, it is assumed that working in a library, by definition, means that you always serve in a "library capacity." To put it another way, a library school graduate might take a job as a researcher for a legislator's office, or a graduate of a master's program in personnel management might take a job in a library; why does the latter statistically qualify one as a "librarian" and the former does not?

The survey's job assignments also give the following breakdowns of the number of graduates who describe their jobs with these particular titles (excerpted here):

Database Management	9
Info Consultant	13
LAN Manager	3
Telecomm	4
Webmaster	22

None of these job titles, held by over 4 percent of the graduates, requires a library degree, yet the mere fact that the job takes place in a library qualifies it as a librarian position even more than a librarian title bestowed outside of the traditional library. Adding this number to the totals for "Vendor" placements and "Other" (usually dot-com) placements brings the total to 105, or over 8 percent of recent graduates. Assuming some overlap between the "type of organization" and the "job assignment," it might be safe to assume that 6–7 percent of post-graduation placements are either outside traditional libraries or outside the areas of traditional library training.

Pooling Resources and Sharing Talent

A recent trip to a top-five school of information and library science yielded some interesting anecdotal results. The "Job Opportunities" folder offered more than 200 job listings in numerous libraries. Not a single listing was for the corporate, library vendor, or dot-com employer segments. This is as much the fault of those entities as it is the library schools; but those schools that go the extra mile to prepare students for work in the private sector ought to do more to forge placement relationships with those companies.

It's interesting that library vendors do not make a bigger play for LIS graduates. Most of the stories one hears of placements with them involve serendipity, luck, or pursuits of last resort. LIS programs bear some of the responsibility for this, but library vendors shoulder the rest of the failure. Moreover, library school graduates should not hide the "second career" potential of their new degrees. Some librarians try to forget the varied path that led them to library school, but the private sector might take notice of these skills.

LIS Job Placement: A Foolish Consistency

In 1975 Margaret Myers, director of the Office for Library Personnel Resources of the ALA, began writing a section on "Free-lance Librarianship" in the "How to Get a Job in Librarianship" section of the *Bowker Annual* (it is now called the "Guide to Employment Sources in the Library and Information Professions"). The exact same text appeared from 1975 to 1980, when the text was broadened. Here is an excerpt from 1984:

> A great deal of interest has been shown in alternative careers and in using information skills in nonlibrary settings. These jobs are usually found through the regular library placement sources, although many library schools are trying to generate such listings for their students and alumni. Job listings that do exist may not specifically call for "librarians" by that title so that ingenuity may be needed to identify jobs where information management skills are necessary.
>
> Some librarians are working on a free-lance basis by offering services to businesses, alternative schools, community agencies, and legislators; these opportunities are usually not found in advertisements but through contacts and publicity over a period of time. A number of information brokering business firms have developed from individual free-lance experiences. Small companies or other organizations often need one-time service for organizing files or collections, bibliographic research for special projects, indexing or abstracting, compilation of directories, and consulting services.
>
> Bibliographic networks and online database companies are using librarians as information managers, trainers, researchers, systems and database analysts, and online service managers. Jobs in this area are sometimes

found in library network newsletters or data processing journals. Classifieds in *Publishers Weekly* may lead to information-related positions. One might also consider reading the Sunday classifieds sections in metropolitan newspapers in their entirety to locate advertisements calling for new information skills under a variety of job titles. Librarians can also be found working in law firms as litigation case supervisors (organizing and analyzing records needed for specific legal cases); with publishers as sales representatives, marketing directors, editors, and computer service experts; and with community agencies as adult education coordinators, volunteer administrators, and grant writers.[3]

A lot has changed in the profession since 1984, except for *Bowker's* opinion on the library job sector, which apparently has not changed at all since 1984. Updated dates and a brief bibliography began to appear in the 1990s, but even after Margaret Myers was no longer responsible for it—beginning in 1995—the text remains largely unchanged from its 1984 version. Here is the same section in the 2001 *Bowker Annual,* seventeen years later (changes from the 1984 version appear in *italics*):

A great deal of interest has been shown *in using information skills in a variety of ways* in nonlibrary settings. These jobs are not usually found through the regular library placement sources, although many library *and information studies programs* are trying to generate such listings for their students and alumni. Job listings that do exist may not call specifically for "librarians" by that title so that ingenuity may be needed to search out jobs where information management skills are needed.

Some librarians are working on a freelance basis, offering services to businesses, alternative schools, community agencies, legislators, *etc.;* these opportunities are usually not found in advertisements but *are created by developing* contacts and publicity over a period of time. A number of information-brokering *businesses* have developed from individual freelance experiences. Small companies or other organizations often need *"one-time"* service for organizing files or collections, bibliographic research for special projects, indexing and abstracting, compilation of directories, and consulting services.

Bibliographic networks and online database companies are using librarians as information managers, trainers, researchers, systems and database analysts, online service managers, *etc.* Jobs in this area are sometimes found in library network newsletters or data processing journals. Librarians can also be found working in law firms as litigation case supervisors (organizing and analyzing records needed for specific legal cases); with publishers as sales representatives, marketing directors, editors, and computer service experts; with community agencies as adult education coordinators, volunteer administrators, grant writers, *etc.*[4]

With the exception of a new proofreading style, and the omission over time of some arguably good advice to read *Publishers Weekly* and the newspaper, there has been no substantial change to this text in seventeen years. The large and steady growth of library vendors is not even mentioned as a possible career alternative. No doubt about it, a master's degree in library science can take you places that traditional library schools and placement services not only never dreamed of, but never intended, either.

THE REVOLVING DOOR
Libraries and Vendors Share Expertise

One of the great benefits of recognizing the coexistence of traditional library job placement with less traditional professional pursuits is the revolving door that stands between the two. Most librarians know someone in the vendor community who has worked for several vendors. It is not uncommon for these professionals to move around the industry—so much so that nondisclosure and noncompetition agreements are now standard in the library automation industry. It is less common, or at least less publicized, when traditional vendors and traditional librarians switch roles. Libraries rarely make a big deal of landing a corporate information professional; nor do library vendors put much stock in hiring traditional librarians for their workforces. This may actually be a positive, since moving back and forth seamlessly should be a goal of the librarian profession.

One thing that libraries and vendors might agree on, however, is that having work experience in a library is especially helpful when working for a library vendor. Merely possessing the perspective of library school might not be enough, barring any other information profession experience, when it comes to taking advantage of a library degree in the private sector. The only tangible advantage is that having the degree puts vendor representatives on a (theoretically) equal footing with the customers to whom they market their services. On the other hand, if library school education prepared students specifically to enter the library vendor marketplace, doing so directly out of library school might not put new graduates at too much of a disadvantage.

Certainly, most software engineers do not work for the companies that buy their software, just as most publishers do not read every book that they sell (beyond the editorial process, of course). It will be interesting to see whether LIS programs begin to couple their course offerings with those in M.B.A. programs. This combination would make an interesting education for those wishing to enter the entrepreneurial side of librarianship—the newest revolving door that some librarians now go through daily, choosing entrepreneurship as a supplement to, rather than a replacement for, library service.

"The position of the librarian-as-entrepreneur is an important one because librarians know best what librarians need." So says Peter McCracken, cofounder of Serials Solutions, a reseller of aggregated journal title lists based in Washington state. John Ganly, assistant director of collections at the New York Public Library's Science, Industry, and Business Library, says of the company, "From my end the pleasure of [working] with this company is that it's easier dealing with someone with a library background." In a somewhat more schizophrenic statement, McCracken notes, "As a librarian and as a vendor I really insist that we do things in ways that I as a librarian would like me as a vendor to do them."[5] There is no reason that the same logic cannot extend to other librarians working in the private sector. One might assume that library vendors hire librarians *because* of their library skills, not despite them. In most areas, these skills are directly applicable in a fashion that serves both the library vendor and the library profession.

Recalling the vendor survey discussed in chapter 1, another question asked vendors to describe their workforce as it relates to traditional notions of the library profession. Here is the excerpted question (the entire survey can be found in appendix B at the end of this book; a list of the vendors to whom the survey was sent is in chapter 1):

(6) How many of your staff are professional librarians? What is the average number of years those professionals have worked in a library?

The numbers reported were surprisingly high:

Total number of employees	3,138
Average number of employees per firm	392
Median number of employees per firm	252
Total number of professional librarians	319
Average number of professional librarians per firm	40
Median number of professional librarians per firm	28

Total years of average library experience per firm   54

Average years of individual library experience   8

Median years of individual library experience   7

According to the vendors themselves, nearly 10 percent of their workforce is made up of librarians. This number far exceeds the 2 percent of recent graduates as reported in the "Placements & Salaries" report in *Library Journal*. Moreover, both the average and median number of years spent working in libraries is most likely enviable by many library personnel and recruitment offices. Library vendors are certainly a force within the profession.

THE PRIVATE SECTOR
The Repurposed M.L.S.

The preface of this book referred to working for a vendor as going to the "dark side." While this is probably the most likely answer that librarians will give for forsaking the lure of corporate culture, there is a more prosaic reason. Libraries, even in times of uncertain funding, are secure, comfortable, relatively even-paced settings. The corporate side of the library world is perceived as a cutthroat, bottom-line, do-or-die career sidetrack. Both of these generalizations are overstated, but based in some truth. Vendors will fire staff for insubordination or nonperformance. A company will stress the bottom line over vaguely stated ethical concerns when push comes to shove. And there is rarely anything resembling tenure in a library automation firm. On the other hand, the pay is often better, there are more opportunities for travel, and performance and rewards are more closely tied.

In an in-depth treatment of library job alternatives, Barbara Herzog lists ten reasons to work for a library vendor:[6]

- You'll be able to serve the library community in an entirely new way, by ensuring that the librarians' point of view is brought to the vendor.
- Colleagues in libraries will become more comfortable in their dealings with vendors who are themselves librarians.
- If travel is something you long for, a number of vendor positions provide such opportunities.
- In many cases, working for a vendor provides you with the opportunity to work with all kinds of libraries.
- The pay is often better than in comparable library positions, while the other benefits are equal.

- Working for a vendor can provide exciting challenges and the opportunity to learn new things while building on library-related knowledge and skills.
- Certain types of positions offer greater flexibility of options for organizing your own time and tasks. This can be useful preparation for those of you who may have an ultimate goal of running your own business.
- If you decide that working for a vendor is not for you, after all, and decide to return to libraries, you'll find that your resume stands out from the rest because of the time you spent working in another milieu.
- Many fewer people apply for these jobs than for attractive library jobs at corresponding levels.
- Finally, a most compelling reason for exploring options in the private sector is the alternative it provides for librarians who have reached a point in their careers where they've become as good at what they do as they can be; that there's little left to learn and that all of the challenges have been met. At this point, most people assume that it's time to move into management. However, for those of you who, like me, realize that library management is not for you, I urge you to think seriously about pursuing opportunities in the private sector as an alternative.

It is not a move to be considered lightly, since tolerance for restructuring and reorganization, extreme flexibility, occasional or frequent travel, and hard work are all traits that library vendors expect.

DOUBLE AGENT
The Library Consultant

In a thinly veiled attempt to create a middle ground between private and library interests, the library consultant was born. Usually possessing strong backgrounds in libraries, this new cadre of seemingly disinterested consultants represents the rationalization of libraryland. Many of these consultants are objective and unbiased, trying to help a wide variety of libraries and working for premium fees that are still lower (usually) than a library gaining the expertise locally. What is generally ignored, however, are the trends created by library consultants. What relationships with vendors do their consulting services usually foster? Which solutions do they ignore because there is no commission, referral fee, or percentage involved? A literature review uncovers little on the subject for the library world, but more and more libraries are ensuring contractually that consultants do not receive payment from any of the sources that provide solutions to the problems the consultants are hired to solve.

In essence, marketing and sales representatives—and even library vendor CEOs—are just a biased version of the library consultant. In some ways, removing the veil of objectivity seems refreshing, in that none of the agendas remain hidden. But library vendors, unlike practically every other field of advertising, tend not to compare themselves to each other. When they do, it is usually tongue in cheek, or wrapped in mysterious references like "be sure to ask the other vendors if they can do X, Y, or Z." You can bet that a Honda dealer will tell you what's wrong with a Ford without couching the language in code. Granted, vendors often do this to inject innuendo and rumors about a rival's product where no hard data exist; however, the overall reluctance to enter into side-by-side comparisons only benefits vendors, and not libraries. Librarians are as reluctant to ask these point-blank questions as well (e.g., "Why does your aggregated data not include journal coverage dates when XYZ's does?"). Instead, the well-known Request for Proposal (RFP) serves as the blunt and benign tool of the trade, gathering piles of data that end up looking the same for every vendor in the marketplace.

Despite their intimate knowledge of the vendor landscape, consultants who have worked for one vendor or another are tainted with questions of bias. Such suspicions of bias, however, would rarely be raised if the consultant had worked for both an academic and a public library, or had worked in a library that used one vendor over another. Why? This notion that working in the nonlibrary private sector taints objectivity more than working in a library has no basis in reality. The truth of the matter is that the library profession includes individuals who work in both libraries and the nonlibrary private sector, both of whom are swayed by internal and external influences throughout the library industry. Calling oneself a consultant should not obviate the need for healthy suspicion among libraries, but the products one has sold in the past don't necessarily taint the path that gets one to a consulting role.

DOT-EDU IN A DOT-COM WORLD

As library and information studies programs struggle for professional and structural stability in this new age of information, many have dropped the "L" word—library—from their titles. This chapter does not intend to enter the debate over what Blaise Cronin calls the "lexical snobbery" with which so many in libraryland take umbrage. Cronin's counterargument to the noted library historian Wayne Weigand in *Library Journal* is noteworthy, however. Weigand had earlier criticized LIS programs for ignoring books and reading in the LIS curricula. Cronin counters that Weigand's "value of stories" is a "manifestly inadequate base upon which to begin to construct a credible discipline, of the kind we these days variously label information science, information management, or information studies." Credible curricula, Cronin concludes, require analytic rigor, not fancy rhetorical defenses of the profession.[7]

The value of content and intimate knowledge of it are slowly being replaced by new technology. In a dot-com world, libraries no longer invent services; they learn the technology that delivers it, and struggle to integrate digital service models into an analog profession. While the Internet is not nearly the panacea that library boards, college chancellors, and local politicians like to think it is, its proliferation and infiltration into the information profession cannot be ignored. This era will undoubtedly reshape the practice, pedagogy, and public perception of the information profession.

As budgetary constraints, strategic initiatives, and widespread LIS program closings from the mid-1980s to the early 1990s forced LIS programs to redefine themselves, so have the potential pools of students and faculty changed. Most of the focus thus far has been on the changing curricula of library schools, but these changes are now bearing their fruits in a new generation of librarians and a new generation of student pools that come to library school. Further attention to the potential of library and information science education can reap even more changes for the better.

Redefining LIS Education

The challenge, as defined by Barbara B. Moran, professor in the School of Information and Library Science at the University of North Carolina at Chapel Hill, comes in serving two masters—the profession and higher education.[8] The attempt to address issues and concerns common to both resulted in two ALA Congresses on Professional Education, in 1999 and 2000; the first dealt with the M.L.S. degree, the second with continuing education. Moran points out that the attention paid to this issue has even caused growing rancor in some camps, but that controversy is still better than disregard.

The profession as a whole must address these educational issues. Library practitioners should do their best to influence LIS curricula to meet the needs of the job market; graduates should support LIS education in their internships, practica, and professional appointments; and faculty need to incorporate changes in the job market—including the growing market for nonlibrary private sector jobs—into the pedagogical structure. On the other side, LIS programs will have to continue to support the master that pays the bills, the university. This raises the issue of competing for academic resources, which is what brought on the LIS redefinition in the first place.

One thing that has not changed much since the advent of library schools is the use of adjunct faculty to teach some of the less theoretical components necessary to join the professional workforce. What LIS programs have rarely explored, however, is leveraging corporate interests to gain valuable resources for LIS education. This is usually done under the guise of educational access to paid databases, complimentary digital content, or reduced fees for conference registration or exhibit passes. Library schools might be able to leverage a lot more from companies that will be marketing their wares to the ranks of library school graduates over the next five to ten years. Finding a way to do this without conflict of interest and on a level playing field presents challenges, but it addresses both the need for outside resources in library schools and the practical application of library resources that must take place regardless of whether a library student is exposed to those resources during his or her time in school.

Vendor and dot-com information industry experts should also be sought-after adjunct faculty. The practical perspectives that they add to the field—as well as the awareness-raising aspects of careers outside of libraries—benefit both existing graduate students and the potential pool of students who might not have otherwise considered library school. The relationship would also expose vendors and corporate representatives to perspectives that they either lost since having worked in libraries or were never in touch with in the first place.

Some libraries are already on the cutting edge of this curriculum shift, and the rest are sure to follow suit. Several schools now offer multiple degree tracks in either library science, information science, or various information technologies. The following examples represent changes and departmental mergers involving traditional library and information science (LIS) programs. Drexel University offers an interdisciplinary degree, cosponsored by the LIS, math, and engineering departments, in software engineering. The University of Pittsburgh's LIS school, in conjunction with the departments of computer science and engineering, offers students a degree in telecommunications. In May 2001, SUNY Buffalo's LIS joined forces with the Department of Communication to launch the School of Informatics, focusing on "the processes of seeking, organizing, evaluating, and communicating information and knowledge."9 The University of Denver offers courses on web content management and competitive intelligence. The University of California at Berkeley was so bold in redefining its LIS program as the School of Information Management and Systems that it did not even seek accreditation from the ALA. Perhaps taking the placement opportunities more seriously, the Palmer School of Library and Information Science in Long Island is now preparing graduates for careers as librarians specifically in corporations, financial institutions, and consulting firms.

The major trend in course development involves user-centered and technology-centered courses. Many of the top twenty schools listed below also offer distance learning courses.[10]

U.S. News and World Report's 1999 Ranking of Library Science Programs

1. (tie) University of North Carolina–Chapel Hill
1. (tie) University of Illinois–Urbana-Champaign
3. (tie) Syracuse University
3. (tie) University of Michigan–Ann Arbor
6. (tie) Indiana University
6. (tie) Rutgers State University–New Brunswick (N.J.)
8. University of Wisconsin–Madison
9. Drexel University (Pa.)
10. (tie) University of California–Los Angeles
10. (tie) University of Texas–Austin
12. (tie) Florida State University
12. (tie) Simmons College (Mass.)
14. University of Maryland–College Park
15. (tie) State University of New York–Albany
15. (tie) University of North Texas
18. (tie) State University of New York–Buffalo
18. (tie) University of Washington
20. (tie) Kent State University (Ohio)
20. (tie) Texas Women's University
20. (tie) University of Tennessee–Knoxville
20. (tie) University of Wisconsin–Milwaukee
20. (tie) Wayne State University (Mich.)

Redefining Potential Student Pools

Redefined curricula are already educating a broader range of undergraduate and postgraduate information professionals. This is the main strategy that has raised the level of awareness of LIS programs on college and university campuses. Now that the Internet bubble has partially burst, refugee librarians from the corporate sector will be looking for work again, perhaps in areas a little more stable, both in pace and salary. Still more dot-com refugees, however, know nothing of library school, and there is nothing like an economic down-turn to send people back to graduate school; LIS programs should capitalize on this new pool of potential students. Traditional LIS coursework, however, is less likely to attract this cadre of Internet professionals; it will take courses in information brokering, electronic publishing, business intelligence, web-mastering, Intranet development, management information systems (MIS), telecommunications, and Internet entrepreneurship.

Distance learning has also helped redefine potential student pools, and offers opportunities to professionals looking to improve their skill sets. Many LIS pro-grams offer distance learning alternatives, and some even allow exclusive off-campus access to their programs. As Carol Tenopir, professor at the School of Information Sciences at the University of Tennessee, Knoxville, states, "Dis-tance learning means more opportunities to earn a degree and—since many of these courses are also open to working information professionals who already have a degree—more opportunities for continuing education."[11]

If in fact LIS programs are missing potential pools of students, then LIS graduates (this author included) are equally guilty of ignoring LIS programs as potential pools of new knowledge. Practicing librarians are often critical of academia for not teaching LIS students what they need to know to survive in libraries. The same cannot be said for the research conducted by LIS faculty. But practitioners rarely turn to faculty research until it winds up in a litera-ture search. Practicing librarians troll electronic discussion lists, perform liter-ature reviews, or attend conferences looking for the latest problem or newest solution, but rarely do they turn to LIS programs or their faculty for direc-tion. If LIS faculty must change the way they teach, LIS graduates should alter the way they learn as well.

Redefining the Role of Paraprofessionals

Paraprofessionals are another underutilized resource in libraries. While many theories likely exist to explain why libraries do not raise and laud the status of library clerks—those in the trenches—here is a rather iconoclastic theory. In a way, library paraprofessionals represent the paradox of libraryland's pro-fessional standing. Deep down, most library professionals know that parapro-fessionals—this includes nonlibrarians working in the nonlibrary private sec-tor that contributes to library services—perform several professional services. They work the reference desk, sit on web design committees, supervise cir-culation activity, run the stacks, deal with vendors, and provide a plethora of raw data that informs professional management's decision making. On the other side of the coin, all professional librarians perform duties broadly described as clerical. Librarians keep statistics, troubleshoot databases, circulate books, process papers, edit web pages, and provide the bulk of data entry that informs either their own or their superiors' professional conclusions.

This is paradoxical, because any recognition that paraprofessionals provide professional services or that librarians perform clerical duties might threaten the image of the profession. More than paradoxical, though, it is ironic, given that the status of information professionals is on the rise, and the distinction made between paraprofessionals and librarians by the average user is nonexistent.

Like any other profession, it is crazy to think that credit hours earned in a classroom do more to shape a profession than 500 hours spent working in a library. Certainly more paraprofessionals would get a degree—the "union card" approach—if it meant that their time served counted toward such an award. And professional practitioners could certainly do more to influence the education that has been slowly pried from their grasp over the last half-century. Philip Turner, dean of the School of Library and Information Sciences at the University of North Texas, argues, "A century ago, most library education was provided in the library by librarians. The concept of a discipline of library science with a cadre of professors teaching library science for a living is a twentieth-century phenomenon. That this would be done at the graduate level in schools devoted entirely to library education is a second-half-of-the-twentieth-century concept."[12]

This is not meant to imply that there is no value in the classroom approach to library science; it adds perspective to the practical application of library service, but in and of itself is not a replacement for actual service in a library. No one wants a doctor who did not go to medical school; on the other hand, library science is hardly medical science. Perhaps some middle ground between raising the status of those in the trenches and humbling the professional status of librarians will improve the situation for both, and mean better service for constituents in the long run. This approach could go well beyond the new practice of recruiting adjunct faculty, usually practitioners, to teach in the classroom. It could mean the introduction of on-the-job training, prolonged internships (including those in the nonlibrary private sector), or what Turner proposes as a cooperative arrangement whereby faculty manage courses and teach theory and principles, while one or more practitioners teach the more volatile portion of course content, like reference resources and technology solutions. Perhaps this notion can even counter the paradoxical nature of professional status described above. If the professional corps contributed more to the professional development of new librarians, that would certainly be a worthy task, and one that is distinct from the performance of clerical and basic service functions.

Redefining the Library Job Market

Imagine how valuable it would be to a library to send its paraprofessionals to work at a library vendor. Imagine getting a help-desk staff member from a library's favorite vendor to spend three months working in a library acquisitions department. Imagine Amazon.com, ebrary, and Questia taking active roles in library conferences, beyond the mere marketing of their products to the industry that helps sustain them. Taking a broader approach to library science student pools necessitates taking a broader approach to the job market that these graduates will enter upon completion of their degrees. It means fostering the relationships between educators and practitioners for the long term, no matter what placement those graduates choose. It means recognizing that the information industry includes a wide array of jobs that library schools never envisioned. It means breaking down the stereotypes of competition and building bonds of collaboration.

Mark Herring, dean of library services at Winthrop University, laments that too many nonlibrarians are planning the library's future from vantage points in dot-coms, digitization projects, and distance education offices.[13] Couple this with the fact that professional librarians tend to ignore the professional capabilities and contributions of those outside the ivory towers and traditional settings of their own profession, and you have the ingredients for waning professional status. Library excellence does not speak for itself, and there are many in the profession who are not being heard.

Like the rest of this book, there are some extreme views presented here, but like most extreme views and suggested radical changes, there is always some middle ground. This chapter points out the major changes that are already taking shape in the library profession, and presents a way to build on some of those changes. Reliance on dot-com and library vendor solutions is already pervasive in every kind of traditional library setting. That these forces don't have more of a presence in library school curricula, faculty, student bases, and job placement services does a disservice to both students and the corporations for whom many students wind up working. Leigh Estabrook, dean of the Graduate School of Library and Information Science at the University of Illinois, sums up one of that school's educational missions this way: "The School's faculty believes strongly that librarianship and newly emerging related fields must be held together to prevent libraries from becoming obsolete and other fields from being unconcerned about issues of access, privacy, and service."[14]

Notes

The first epigraph for this chapter is a quotation of Joel Summerlin, a graduate of the Information School at the University of Washington who works as a thesaurus lead at Corbis, Inc. He was quoted in Norman Oder, "2000 Grad Joel Summerlin: New Orders," *Library Journal* 126, no. 17 (2001): 38.

The second epigraph is a quotation of Linda Feist, who holds an M.L.S. degree from the University of Chicago. She was quoted in Linda K. Wallace, "Places an MLS Can Take You," *American Libraries* 33, no. 3 (2002): 44.

1. Tom Terrell and Vicki L. Gregory, "Plenty of Jobs, Salaries Flat," *Library Journal* 126, no. 17 (2001): 34–40.
2. Terrell and Gregory, "Plenty of Jobs," 34 (emphasis added).
3. Julia Ehresmann, ed., *The Bowker Annual of Library and Book Trade Information,* 29th ed. (New York: R. R. Bowker, 1984), 304.
4. Dave Bogart, ed., *Bowker Annual: Library and Book Trade Almanac,* 46th ed. (New Providence, N.J.: R. R. Bowker, 2001).
5. Norman Oder, "Peter McCracken: Librarian as Entrepreneur," *Library Journal* 126, no. 13 (2001): 44.
6. Betty-Carol Sellen, ed., *What Else Can You Do with a Library Degree* (New York: Neal–Schuman, 1997), 76.
7. Blaise Cronin, "The Dreaded 'L' Word," *Library Journal* 126, no. 5 (2001): 58. Weigand quoted within. Weigand's original criticism appeared in *Chronicle of Higher Education* (Oct. 27, 2000).
8. Barbara B. Moran, "Practitioners vs. LIS Educators: Time to Reconnect," *Library Journal* 126, no. 18 (2001): 54.
9. *Library Journal* (May 2001).
10. Carol Tenopir, "I Never Learned That in Library School," *Online* 24, no. 2 (2000): 46. Reprinted from the *U.S. News and World Report* graduate school ranking.
11. Tenopir, "I Never Learned That," 46.
12. Philip M. Turner, "Library and Information Studies: Education in the Age of Connectivity" (presentation given at the Texas Library Association, March 25, 1997). Available at http://www.txla.org/pubs/tlj-4q96/turner.html (visited April 2002).
13. Mark Y. Herring, "Our Times, They Are a–Changin', But Are We?" *Library Journal* 126, no. 17 (2001): 44.
14. Quoted in Tenopir, "I Never Learned That," 43.

6 | LIBRARIES ARE NOT *ALL* BUSINESS

The title of this chapter represents the double-edged sword that sets libraries apart from their corporate counterparts. That libraries are not all business makes them attractive, but it also makes them vulnerable when dealing with entities that have cadres of M.B.A.s, lawyers, and business professionals. So many challenges face libraries that it is often difficult to take a step back and form the strategies that will allow libraries to challenge businesses, or at least posit themselves as viable alternatives to commercial information services. Libraries do not generally play hardball; nor are they particularly good at marketing strategies. And while national organizations like the ALA, Public Library Association, Special Libraries Association, and the Association of Research Libraries (ARL) go to great lengths to give professional librarians philosophical legs to stand on, their collective bite is seldom greater than their bark. Furthermore, not only are there several philosophical and tangible issues on which libraries should be challenging library vendors and commercial entities; in some instances, solutions even exist.

LICENSING AND FAIR USE

Recall the earlier discussion of how the keyword search clouded the imagination of librarians and vendors for almost two decades of online catalog development; the discovery opportunities offered by the simple full-record search staggered librarians for so long that they were nearly blind to the utility of any other new feature. In a similar fashion, libraries have been blinded for the last ten years by the widespread proliferation of electronic full-text journals and databases. Those with the resources bought full text as fast as it was made available, signing licenses faster than an attorney could read page one of the use agreements contained therein. Having bought the proverbial pig in a poke, libraries are just now beginning to question some of the language in those licenses, but often it is too late.

The Kidnapping of Fair Use

None of this should suggest some sinister plot to dupe libraries into a false sense of security, or to bait-and-switch them into agreements that begin cheap and end up costing a fortune (although that happens as well, most notably Elsevier's token-purchase plan for online content in ScienceDirect—several libraries were first offered free tokens for access to data that was not available through the base subscription; those tokens now cost libraries dearly). Most online resource vendors entered the arena with a naiveté matched only by their librarian counterparts. But vendors certainly got smarter faster, and libraries that failed to pay attention are worse off for it.

It's probably safe to say that most publishers are not particular fans of the "fair use doctrine," the stated exception to the U.S. copyright act that allows for limited and educational use of copyrighted materials without compensation to the copyright holder. In decades past, libraries have attempted to educate users about fair use and the fine line that exists between it and plagiarism or theft. With the advent of digital text came an opportunity for publishers to take their revenge on fair use, by applying digital technology—usually referred to collectively as "digital rights management" (DRM)—to monitor, restrict, and control the use of digital materials. The Association of American Publishers has a long history of affirming that fair use is not a right, but merely a defense to copyright infringement. With DRM, the publishing industry has its tool for quashing that so-called right for good. Moreover, much DRM development has occurred in the wake of the Napster fiasco, which had users pirating music files and sharing them anonymously across an amorphous network of local computers. Almost all of this DRM development has taken place without the input of publishers' major bulk buyers, libraries.

Moreover, digital licensing agreements are now generally understood to act as contracts—contracts that override the provisions of fair use. These contracts, signed by thousands of libraries, now govern the use of online materials. If such a contract has no provision for fair use contained in it, then the contractual obligation trumps any fair use defense. With the exception of some law libraries, not too many libraries have attorneys on staff, and even those that do rarely empower them to act as such over campus or local jurisdictional attorneys. Suddenly, the simple signing of a contract to put digital full text within reach of library users is in danger of becoming a long, drawn-out, adversarial process.

If the library does have a lawyer involved with the licensing procedure, it might be a good idea for the library to inform him or her which aspects of the contract mean the most to the library.[1] First, determine how patrons will need to use the online resource; this will make contrary language stand out before one even reads the license agreement. Consideration of how a digital resource is used includes remote access needs, simultaneous users, premise restrictions, printing capabilities, etc. Second, determine whether fair use is permitted or overridden by the license. Third, the library should know its price and the elements of the license that it is willing to sacrifice and which it is not. Fourth, the library should know the individual, or at least the company, with whom it is dealing. Fifth, take nothing for granted. If the license is unclear about remote access, then clarify it and get the language inserted in the agreement. Finally, be assertive, including knowing when to walk away from a negotiation. If a lot of time invested takes the negotiation nowhere, chances are that continuing without a long break will be just as fruitless. An assertive—but not aggressive—stance is especially crucial, since the library does not walk away from the table owning the content. This is not like buying a car, after which one can do with it as one pleases. The license agreement is just that—the right to use the material under the static (yet renewable) conditions of the agreement. This brings the library to the second important departure of the information age.

OWNERSHIP VS. ACCESS

If libraries could save 50 percent on the price of every book just by returning it to the publisher after five years, would they do it? Probably not, in most cases. Then why are libraries willing to pay 150 percent of the value of print for an electronic version of something that they do not even own once they have access to it? Before the Internet, it would have been unheard of for libraries to spend millions of dollars on content that they would never take possession of. In the earlier days of automation, CD-ROMs added the sense of comfort that comes with physical ownership. Now CD-ROMs are traded for web access faster than one can say "www." This might not be an issue for libraries that use online access merely as a supplement to print editions of data, but for the rest of the content that libraries lease, there should be a contingency plan when the relationship with the online vendor comes to a mutual (or otherwise) end.

Outsourcing Data Warehousing

The last two decades of literature in library science have devoted a lot of time and space to the dreaded "O" word—outsourcing. The profession, in an effort to keep costs down, began sending some of its most traditional work to jobbers: binding, cataloging, labeling, etc. There is much less mention, however, of outsourcing library data. Libraries show great concern when books from the stacks must go into remote storage, or, to use more politically correct terms, the library annex, satellite shelving facility, or local compact shelves. But when it comes to data, libraries' attitudes to ownership and access suddenly change. The longevity, trustworthiness, and financial stability of online vendors are regularly taken for granted.

One solution is to own the data itself. Rather than license it, actually make an agreement with a vendor that includes the local maintenance of software and of the storage of online data. This is not as difficult as it was formerly, with the prices of disk space decreasing at the rate of Moore's Law. Libraries, however, may like their technological outsourcing alternative just fine, and several vendors will most likely not offer such an option anyway. There are other solutions, then, that fall squarely on the vendor.

1. *Ensure that all the data and software are escrowed.* Libraries do not want to find themselves in a situation where their online data is taken away from them simply because the company that provided it has become insolvent. Access agreements should include provisions that allow continuing access to the data, at the very least, and ideally to the software used to access and view that data.

2. *Demand that vendors describe their own disaster-preparedness plans.* Are library vendors performing regular backups? Are libraries sure? Recent history tells us that dramatic disasters can happen when no one suspects them. Libraries should avoid surprises when disaster strikes hundreds, or even thousands, of miles away.

3. *Ownership provisions.* Libraries might want to insert access provisions that would include taking ownership of licensed data when the relationship

with the vendor ends. JSTOR includes such a provision in its agreements. Libraries should also receive details regarding exactly how such a data hand-off would take place.

A Backup Is Not an Archive

Most vendors would admit, when pressed, that archiving digital data is not their strong suit. Most libraries, for that matter, still grapple with the difficult task of ensuring long-term access to their own digitally born and stored data. When the dreaded day comes that a vendor ships three terabytes of data to the library, make sure that the data are retrievable and usable, and are not simply a pile of backup tapes, a simple snapshot in time. Libraries should also ensure that the vendor has maintained the integrity of the data, and that appropriate descriptions for them, called administrative metadata, accompany the raw data files. Administrative metadata can consist of details about the software used to create the electronic file, dots-per-inch scanning specifications, and specifics about the metadata standards used to tag textual data.

This is a difficult area for libraries to challenge their vendors, for two reasons: (1) libraries are still in the process of determining the best practices for the storage and long-term preservation of digital materials; and (2) library and data vendors cannot make profits from the costly enterprise of digital preservation. This might mean an opportunity for third-party preservationists to partner with libraries and vendors to ensure the security and integrity of all the online data on which libraries have become dependent to serve their users, and which vendors rely on for their livelihoods. The point is that there exists a mutually beneficial solution that meets the needs of all parties.

Left Holding the Virtual Bag

Even this author is willing to admit that elements of this data ownership scenario are pie-in-the-sky. Not until a major library is left holding the empty digital bag will this issue show its full effects. Somewhere, right now, there is data that will be lost and gone forever in the next five to ten years. Who knows? It may have already disappeared. When that day comes, will patrons blame a nameless, faceless vendor, or will they blame the libraries that they believe to be the guardians of information?

HOW TO MAKE VENDORS LISTEN

Perhaps the most difficult part of all of this is getting vendors to listen to suggestions that cost them a lot and earn them nothing. In many cases, vendors are not as beholden to the library customer as libraries are obligated to their patrons to continue providing access to valuable materials. This makes it hard to put library vendors over a barrel. The philosophical aspects of ensuring access well into the future do not appeal to them. More often than not, vendors spend more time and effort improving web interfaces and adding features than they do thinking about the actual data that their databases contain.

Vendor-Library Integration and Partnership

Efforts in this area will require the concerted support of both libraries and vendors, most likely with some sort of mutual back-scratching agreement. Perhaps major libraries could agree to serve as the escrow repositories for important digital resources, in much the same way that JSTOR was born. Perhaps joint grant and vendor funding would support such efforts. Vendors, too, could be more vocal about the sorts of things that libraries could provide them with to make their businesses more profitable. This might take the form of reporting circulation statistics to publishers so that they can determine trends in readership or uncover holes in title backlists. These data might even be provided on a national scale, if libraries could agree collectively on how to collect, tabulate, and distribute them.

Libraries also need to play the "standards" card whenever possible. Library vendors know all too well how much their customers appreciate adherence to standards. Mutual partnerships in this regard tend to benefit libraries a little bit more, since determining how much of a role standards play in vendor selection is difficult to determine. Such partnership initiatives are difficult when a particular vendor has a monopoly in a given area, but in a lot of cases, vendors realize that their wares—whether technology or content—are available from alternative sources; if libraries flock, collectively, to vendors who adhere to standards, then the message is clear. Two specific recent developments show that vendors are listening.

The first example involves the difficult realm of library statistics. If there is one thing that libraries love as much as standards, it's statistics. It is amazing that it has taken this long for the library community to put the two together. To date, no standard exists for the compilation, delivery, or reporting of statistics for the use of electronic resources in libraries. The ARL is in the process of evaluating its statistical requests in this area, and was quickly alerted to the fact that vendors—even those that provide statistics—fail to do so in any standardized way. This makes meaningful analysis between products, and between libraries, extremely difficult. The ARL's E-Metrics initiative (http://www.arl.org/stats/newmeas/emetrics) is an effort to explore the feasibility of defining and collecting data on the use and value of electronic resources. The initial investigations and testing have brought several vendors to the table interested in making the collaborative effort worthwhile.

The second example of collaboration involves the new NISO Circulation Interchange Protocol (NCIP). This fledgling standard will define various transactions needed to support circulation activities among independent library systems. Think of this as Z39.50 for circulation. As of the spring of 2002, the National Information Standards Organization (NISO) had released the NCIP as a draft standard for trial use. Interestingly, adoption of the standard will require a great deal of cooperation in the traditionally proprietary and competitive field of ILS vendors. Even more interestingly, the chair of the standards committee and the Standards Development Committee liaison are both from the vendor community—Patricia Stevens of OCLC, and Mark Needleman of the Sirsi Corporation. The entire committee is made up of a mix of vendors and library representatives.

Enhancements Are Profitable

Libraries and vendors might together determine the best way to market new services, or the best prices to put on the ownership of data and archival services. Even if the price was dear, assurance that at least one library or consortium was paying it would go a long way toward ensuring the peace of mind of the library community and the profitability of online vendors. In the case of statistics, for example, providing standardized statistical measures might be an added cost item and hence a profit incentive for vendors. For vendors that provide these statistical measures, it might mean obtaining from libraries more tangible data about the use of their product, and thus result in more revenue from continued subscriptions and word of mouth.

In the case of the NCIP, vendors who jump onto the bandwagon of a new protocol will be able to market their company's support for, or compliance with, the new standard. This makes their product more profitable and easier to market in a multisystem environment, which is just about *every* environment.

Point Out Their Flaws

One of the questions put to library vendors in the survey referred to in chapter 1 was what kind of feedback mechanisms the vendor supported, and whether customers used them. Every vendor that responded gave examples of feedback mechanisms, and most reported that customers used them with great frequency. Libraries could use these feedback channels for a concerted effort to point out vendor systems' flaws in a detailed and standardized way. The use of screen shots, analysis by local design experts, and usability testing make the job of improving interfaces and services easier for the vendor, and ultimately serve the library.

In other instances, library vendors, both technology- and content-driven ones, put themselves into relationships that jeopardize their standing in the library community. When they do this, sometimes with tremendous naiveté, libraries should point out the negative impact such relationships have on their reputation. For example, how complicit are full-text database vendors in the rising costs of online serials? Is the full text that they make available through their databases making direct access more expensive? When scholarly organizations partner with content aggregators, bypassing direct access by their members, are they doing a disservice to the organization and the scholarly community? On the other hand, librarians need to be reminded of the same issue from time to time, as the librarians on the advisory board to Questia found out through a vocal professional backlash.

WHAT IF VENDORS WON'T LISTEN?

The adversarial position that libraries find themselves in is often due to the monopoly status of the vendor. If someone owns data that no one else owns, then they can rightly charge what the market will bear. Regardless of how high the price a vendor might place on its monopoly commodity, libraries would rarely find themselves in a position to bargain for more access, more features, or better licensing. In this case, libraries might use collective boycotts in order to force vendors to change their strategy. A good example of this recently played out with academic libraries' access to *Nature* magazine online. After months of debate over the terms of archival access to materials and the embargoing of recent issues, *Nature* changed its policy and opened up what had been very closed and fierce negotiations with libraries.[2]

The debate over *Nature* has extended itself to other titles, such as *Science,* and to publishers in their entirety, who now see a real threat of competition among the producers of scholarly content (as discussed in the "Scholarly Initiatives vs. High Profit" section of chapter 1). More often, however, in the business of Internet information, the business entity neither knows nor cares that the library exists. This poses a provocative, but inspiring, challenge to libraries.

Positioning Libraries to Take Over

Traditionally, libraries have always been able to handle challenges from information sources outside their realm of control. This was easy when libraries could decide not to collect a book or magazine, but the advent of the Web—and a user population that does not distinguish between a web-based journal and a homegrown website—has increased the challenge exponentially. While the democratic nature of the Web makes it impossible, if not unethical, for libraries to eradicate unauthorized sources of information, there *is* something libraries can do to cope: they can spend as much time on the Web as possible and learn as much as possible about competing forces.

User education just might be the best weapon libraries have to compete with duplicitous, disingenuous, monopolistic, and parasitic Internet businesses. If Questia can send e-mails to students' parents encouraging a paid subscription, then libraries should be able to do the same, describing the dubious nature of such content, and stressing the fact that an even better experience awaits them at even the most basic undergraduate library. If Google can offer online reference-question assistance for a price, then libraries should endeavor to spread the word about equivalent free services. If patrons would rather Ask Jeeves than ask a librarian, then libraries should consider the strength of that branding and marketing model.

Copy, Copy, Copy

Rather than moan and groan every time a company bases a new online business model on an old library service, libraries might do their best to compare their traditional service with the new one. Libraries might consider hiring—either full time or part time—more technical staff to replicate the most popular bells and whistles available at these corporate sites. If Marsh Technologies can master book printing, cutting, and binding on demand with PerfectBook, then why aren't libraries buying? Despite increasing demand and the patrons' proven preference for full-text databases, few libraries have initiated print-on-demand services. Amazon and other online retailers brag about the savings they offer their customers, but libraries rarely analyze the cost savings that they themselves pass on to patrons. (See figures 6-1 and 6-2.) Perhaps a concerted effort to prove the value of information to patrons will make them use the library's resources even more. While this would not necessarily change the price of the resources, it would certainly increase their value.

Com+ Developer's Reference Library (Windows Programming Reference Series)
by David Iseminger

List Price: ~~$149.99~~
Our Price: **$104.99**
You Save: $45.00 (30%)

SAVE $45.00 **LOWER PRICES!**

Used Price: **$38.99**

FIGURE 6-1   Amazon.com reminds its customers how much they are saving.

Com+ Developer's Reference Library (Windows Programming Reference Series)
by Andrew Pace

List Price: $149.99
Processing Price: $46.25
Total Price: 196.24
Your Price: $0.00

LOWEST PRICES!   You save 100%

FIGURE 6-2   This fictitious replica of the Amazon savings statement could show patrons the value of using the library.

Libraries will never be completely like businesses, nor should they be. The characteristics that set libraries apart from corporate interests can do libraries harm, but they can also work to their advantage, as the next chapter will show.

Notes

1. Most of this advice is taken from a nicely condensed article by Lesley Ellen Harris. The advice is not meant to be exhaustive. See Lesley Ellen Harris, "Deal-Maker, Deal-Breaker: When to Walk Away," *Library Journal Netconnect* (2000): 12–14.

2. Embargoing involves limiting access to recent issues of a journal for a period of time until the publisher decides to release the content. For example, the most recent issue of an online journal might not be available until the print version has circulated for three months. Even though the library is paying full price, patrons must wait due to contractual obligations set by the publisher. The debate over *Nature* and how several libraries dealt with it is covered in great detail at http://www.ub.uni-stuttgart.de/ejournals/Nature_andere_Univ.html.

7 FIRST PRINCIPLES

Patron Privacy, Anonymity, and Confidentiality

We protect each library user's right to privacy and confidentiality with respect to information sought or received and resources consulted, borrowed, acquired or transmitted.
—Principle III, ALA "Code of Ethics," 1995

It may have once been true that on the Internet no one knew you were a dog . . . these days marketers probably know your favorite brand of dog food.
—Josh Dubeuman and Michael Beaudet

In nearly any profession, first principles—the ethics, guidelines, and rules on which a profession is built—serve as a professional benchmark by which the leaders of the vocation judge their success and failure, assess their history, and guide their future. Most of this book deals with a perceived need to shift those principles, bending them in places that serve library users, and breaking them in places of severe stress. These shifts are presented in comparison with the service models and information delivery of various corporate entities. This chapter, however, addresses one ethical topic that libraries cannot ignore, and which stands in stark contrast to the majority of corporate business models. Moreover, when faced with it, libraries should not surrender to business practices, or, if they do, they should at least acquiesce with full disclosure and extreme caution.

ERODING EXPECTATIONS OF PRIVACY

In a setting long forgotten by this author, an Internet ethicist mused that the biggest challenge facing Internet privacy is a culture in which most Americans would surrender a DNA sample in return for a McDonald's Extra Value Meal. In this light, convincing library patrons of the importance of maintaining their own privacy is extremely challenging, if not impossible. Moreover, the primary area in which libraries have touted privacy ethics is the patron borrowing record; it represents the Rock of Gibraltar around which all of the profession's opinions on privacy revolve. In this chapter it is assumed—perhaps to the point of overgeneralizing—that the profession holds sacred this particular right to confidentiality. For some reason, though, this standard by which a library's stance on privacy is so often judged does not easily extend to digital services outside the realm of the patron record database. Moreover, the sacred cow of the patron record itself is in danger of collapsing under the weight of personalization features and the conflict between the confidentiality of personal data and the convenience of personal service over the Web.

Before the Internet, libraries needed only to assure patrons that their privacy would be preserved to the fullest extent possible. Two important developments have shifted the character of this tradition from a professional courtesy to an educational imperative. The first is libraries' growing reliance on outsourced information vendors, who, under the guise of personalization, offer services in exchange for personal information. The second is the proliferation of local digital services which libraries fail to hold up to the same standard as the traditional patron record, and for which libraries are sacrificing privacy.

Informational Privacy

Michael Gorman defines informational privacy as the "right to control personal information and to hold our retrieval and use of information and recorded knowledge to ourselves."[1] Library professional organizations do not talk much about privacy, at least not as much as they talk about the evils of web filtering and censorship. This is not to find fault with either the lack of attention to former, or the needed attention to the latter, but merely to point out the sticky nature of the privacy debate, especially since it could potentially mean a lot of work for libraries if librarians thought seriously about complying with their profession's standards of protecting privacy in the age of the Internet. Technology, in both its use by librarians to leverage much-needed functionality, and in its easy adoption by library patrons, focuses serious concerns on the right to privacy.

This chapter does not intend to debate whether or not a right to privacy exists or is deserved by patrons. It should suffice that privacy is part of the ethical standard which libraries uphold. This standard is a part of the profession, even if it is not supported by the natural or literal law of the land; liberal or conservative politics aside, adherence to patron privacy and confidentiality is a cornerstone of the profession. Libraries, especially public and academic ones, might take this a step further by stating that library patrons not only have an explicit right to privacy, they have an implicit right to anonymity. For any library activity that does not require personal identification—browsing, reading, database searching, public web terminal usage—patrons should be able to assume anonymous access to materials; when library activities do require identification—circulation, database log-ins, credit card transactions—patrons should be assured of their privacy.

User Profiling

One of the frustrations recently eased by information technology is the ability of automated customer services to recognize the users of a particular service. In an age where most public rest rooms have sinks and toilets that recognize one's presence, it is increasingly infuriating to use a computer every day that has no way of knowing who is sitting in front of it, or that anyone is sitting in front of it at all. Websites are now becoming capable of such recognition services once a user's presence is announced. This is not meant to be a prolonged dead horse-beating of the much-maligned web "cookie," the technology that stores local information about log-ins, browsing habits, and so on in an effort to simplify web browsing and customize content. The debate over cookies, and the near-paranoid frenzy of fear over this technology, have already done the damage of stunting the adoption of simple technologies in libraries. Perhaps it was easier for librarians to display a knee-jerk reaction to a technology that they did not understand, while they simultaneously began the wholesale outsourcing of patron privacy through benign neglect.

Avoiding the cookie debate entirely, the focus on user profiling has to do with online services that are increasingly turning to personalized services by way of current awareness managers, search alerts, table of contents servers, and personal resources lists. (See figure 7-1.) The examples are almost too numerous to mention. Almost every major library content provider has some sort of personalized content-delivery mechanism in place.

Rarely do these services request any descriptive information that differs greatly from that contained in the traditional library patron record; the departure comes in linking that personal information with personal preferences, such as professional discipline, research areas, favorite titles, favorite authors, or even favorite Library of Congress Subject Headings. This is the sort of data that libraries have always been quite careful not to keep about patrons. Next to an obsession with censorship, privacy protection remains the cornerstone of the profession, at least in theory. It is rare to find a library website that warns patrons about trading privacy for online features; fewer still admonish patrons to seek out privacy statements on outside resources. Certainly, most patrons never give the surrender of their private data a second thought; others, however, might assume that a library would not conduct business with a vendor who would take that privacy for granted. Others, still, might transfer their contempt for requests for their personal information to the library that has not made an effort to insure their privacy.

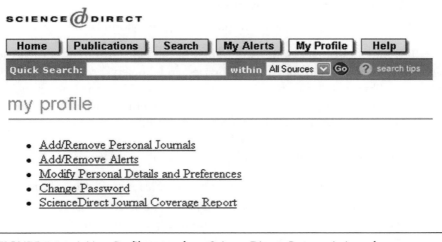

FIGURE 7-1   A User Profile setup from ScienceDirect. By permission of ScienceDirect. © 2002, ScienceDirect. All rights reserved.

PROTECTING PRIVACY

It is up to libraries to decide whether they will act as the ultimate guardians of privacy, and up to patrons to decide how much of that right they are willing to give up for the sake of convenience. Nevertheless, libraries should not simply bury their heads in the sand of ubiquitous web access, expressing dismay at the ignorant forfeiture of privacy by a populace that does not know any better. Self-education is the first concern; after that, libraries can determine to what degree they want to make themselves players in the realm of information privacy.

The following is a short list of the many online resources available on Internet privacy:[2]

ALA Washington Office–Privacy—http://www.ala.org/washoff/ privacy.html

CDT Privacy Issues—http://www.cdt.org/privacy

CNET Features—http://coverage.cnet.com/Content/Features/Dlife/ Privacy

Electronic Frontier Foundation—http://www.eff.org

Electronic Privacy Information Center—http://www.epic.org

P3P Public Overview—http://www.w3.org/P3P

Privacy Foundation—http://www.privacyfoundation.org

Privacy.org—http://www.privacy.org

Privacy Rights Clearinghouse—http://www.privacyfoundation.org

Too much of library policy still resides in the ivory tower, or ends at the completion of the introductory "Libraries and Society" course in library school. A library that fails to educate its staff about library privacy policies, especially paraprofessional staff without the benefit of indoctrination in library ethics, might as well have no policies. Only in this way can users remain truly informed and educated.

Ethical guidelines for information professionals include:

ALA "Code of Ethics"— http://www.ala.org/alaorg/oif/ethics.html

Association of Independent Information Professionals (AIIP) "Code of Ethical Business Practice"—http://www.aiip.org/purethics.html

ASIST Professional Guidelines— http://www.asis.org/AboutASIS/ professionalguidelines.html

User Education

Some libraries go so far as to include bibliographic instruction for patrons in signing up for personalized online services. This is about as far as most libraries will go in including some sort of warning about the personalization-privacy tradeoff that occurs almost daily on the Web. Common practice among frequent web users usually even includes the maintenance of a dummy e-mail account which users will employ any time an unverified website requests an e-mail address. Fear of spam, it seems, is still greater than fear of privacy loss, though the two are loosely tied. Libraries could do even more to protect the privacy of their patrons without losing the benefits of outside-party personalization services.

While the endeavor might seem expensive from a resources point of view, libraries might consider harvesting and repackaging personalized services, in order to ensure that patron data never reaches an entity outside the library. For instance, libraries might collect the table of contents data for certain journal titles and then redistribute them to patrons who have profiled themselves through the library, rather than directly with the vendor. This alternative, which would give private information only to those dedicated to protecting it, both extends the existing service to the patron and reminds him or her that the library is there to protect privacy and ensure anonymity.

Another challenge for systems librarians might entail collecting search criteria for different databases, and then passing the searches to those databases for current awareness purposes. This is the same activity that the vendors themselves conduct when offering the service to patrons, the only difference being that patrons would no longer have to profile themselves on the remote resource. Moreover, patrons profiling through the library would only need to do so once, rather than several times for several different vendors. By acting as the broker in the personalization service, libraries enhance service while insuring privacy.

LIBRARY PRIVACY VIOLATIONS
Alive and Well

While it is tempting to blame technology for the ill treatment that privacy has received of late, technology in and of itself is merely a tool. The driver, not the car, is to blame for road rage. On the other hand, libraries before automation were indeed better about protecting privacy, since the manual systems, such as linking borrower cards with circulation cards (a paper transaction that was forever erased at its end), eliminated the mere possibility of reestablishing links between borrower and content. Despite fears of experts reestablishing deleted borrowing transactions, some libraries are already practicing what can either loosely or determinedly be defined as privacy violations. That the technology allows it is no excuse for the ethical transgression.

Borrower Histories

Even the least sophisticated integrated library system supports several circulation functions that meet the needs of circulation staff. Library vendors did not dream up these features, they came as demands from libraries themselves. For instance, a system might keep track of a book's previous borrower, in case damage to the book is determined after the book is discharged. Is cost recovery worth the privacy violation? Several librarians and vendors have seen circulation clerks ooh and aah during a circulation module demonstration that shows the ability to view fine histories for delinquent borrowers. Does the right to privacy end when the material becomes overdue? Is this punishment for the other borderline ethical practice of labeling patrons as "bad?" It's unlikely that a library would include in its privacy policy a clause that relinquishes the right to patrons who disobey due dates.

Granted, the idea of complete anonymity in patron transactions is a near impossibility. The self-check machine, however, might be remarketed as such a privacy device, especially in light of the (anecdotal and unproven) notion that a circulation clerk would cost the library less money than these technological expenses. But just as patrons latch on to a device that protects the sanctity of their borrowing habits, even from the circulation clerk who might share a class, a neighborhood, or a social circle with them, other patrons are just as happy to forgo privacy for the smallest conveniences.

Just as certainly as Amazon.com keeps track of every transaction a customer makes (as well as visits, searches, browsing habits, and preferences), library patrons are certain to request such features from their local library. For instance, picture the professor who cannot recall the book that she had checked out last semester, other than the fact that it was blue and had a picture of a whale on the verso of the title page. If Amazon, Blockbuster, and Tower Records can remind her of her transaction histories, then why not the library? The overgeneralized explanation—that the ability to do so would make it possible to do so for anyone when requested by law enforcement— is likely to miss its mark with most patrons. "You mean you can't tell me what I checked out in case the government wants to know what an accused criminal has checked out?" Like the user profiling described above, libraries' embrace of new features like this should be made cautiously and with the full disclosure to and signed acceptance of the library patron. Variance from the right of privacy should be the exception, and not the rule.

Web and Library Application Logs

While many library systems work automatically to eradicate borrowing activity, often with little thought given to the matter, the same cannot be universally said of library web use. Web logs are not generally considered repositories of highly sensitive material, but careful examination, extraction, and cross-tabulation with other logs might release information that would surprise the average librarian. For instance, a single log file or various combinations of cross-tabulated log files might show:

- The exact machine from which a web request was made
- A patron's ID and a list of all the titles renewed
- A list of materials requested from interlibrary loan
- A list of all the databases searched on any given day

This is not meant as a scare tactic, since the consistent and careful use of web and application log data can greatly benefit libraries, and not merely for marketing purposes. For example, ILS application and web logs might report, while maintaining anonymity of users, the number of searches in a given index, or the number of searches that resulted in no hits for the user. On the other hand, log files retained in their raw form might be used to link activity to specific users, whether or not the library intends to ever do so. It is as much a shame for libraries to dispose of log files without mining them as it is to maintain and store them without any sort of policy regarding their use and retention. Moreover, most libraries do not have policies regarding the log retention of the vendors with whom they do business. Does the online publisher adhere to the same patron privacy standards as the library? It is unlikely. Staying informed about such policies and seeking information on vendor transgressions in the area of privacy should inform library decision making.

Any number of log analyzers—applications that parse and mine the data from standardized web logs—will extract data from library web logs for administrative, developmental, or system troubleshooting use. Libraries should seriously consider log-retention policies that ensure the translation of library web and application logs into meaningful data, while assuring patrons that private information will not be retained beyond its immediate, short-term usefulness.

Can libraries really answer "no" to this question posed by the ALA in the *Newsletter on Intellectual Freedom?*

Do public and academic libraries monitor library users?

No. Librarians are aware of the behavior of library users and when faced with disruptions or clear violations of the law, they take appropriate action. If laws are broken—as with theft or other violations—the librarian reports this immediately. On the other hand, librarians do not police what library users read or access in the library. Libraries ensure the freedom to read, to view, to speak, and to participate. They are the cornerstones of democracy.[3]

Privacy and Security

One of the most popular features on library websites these days is the ability to look up one's own patron record and renew books. Other libraries offer material holds, requests, and paging from the online catalog, once the patron has gained authenticated access to the service. Most patrons provide the private data requested for these features since they see no harm or possible privacy infringement by anyone who might obtain their library identification; after all, no one can steal an identity, ruin credit, or bill a user's account with a simple library card ID. But just because most patrons have diminished concern for their own privacy, libraries should not extend that lack of concern to all patrons and to all library services tied to this model of authentication. The use of "secure socket layer" (SSL) transactions encrypts the data sent from one server to another without requiring that the data on either end be encrypted itself. The debate over such authentication has been clouded by endless debates over use of the browser BACK button on public workstations and how the caching of private data is handled; despite the importance of that security piece, no library vendor ought to have the audacity to offer patron-initiated services without a model for secure transmission of that patron data.

Some libraries have even begun receiving requests for access to online data via SSL. While secure connections are usually preserved for the transmission of credit card or other sensitive information, offering secure research services may be a new service worth investigation by libraries. While it's difficult to find online data services that offer SSL connections, it is even more unlikely to find one that offers its e-mail alerting service through encrypted or private e-mail networks. This popular feature of e-mail delivery is entirely unsecured. Moreover, several libraries offer services that have HTML FORM submissions, which result in a scripted "send mail" function, sending e-mail with the FORM data to library staff. The privacy concern here is even greater, since the e-mail transmission is not disclosed to the library patron.

Distance Learners

Most libraries also offer some sort of remote access to much of their paid subscription data. In order to avoid distribution, tracking, and periodic changing of library passwords, several libraries (especially academic ones) have opted for the more favorable IP address recognition. Simply put, this allows content servers to determine whether or not the request is coming from an authorized computer. This model breaks down, however, when an authorized user tries to access data from an unauthorized IP domain. This scenario, while not exclusive to them, is best personified in the case of the distance learner. These (usually) remote users pay as much, if not more, tuition than the average campus user, have similar course requirements, and are graded on the same scale, but have direct access to much less material. This usually means that distance learners have to go an extra mile to assure information providers, libraries included, that they have authorization to access library materials.

Libraries have combated the remote access problem by combining the IP recognition offered by online subscription services with something called proxy, or remote access, authentication. Proxy servers authenticate users, by various means, and then pass requests to data servers as if the user is coming from an authorized IP address. One of the nicest things about the proxy model is that the library, not the vendor, is responsible for authenticating the user and validating his right to access the data resource in question. This is a welcome departure from online services such as netLibrary, ebrary, and Questia that require local patron accounts in order to access data. The major factor, then, that distinguishes remote users from local users is the requirement that distance learners must still identify themselves before they can begin their research. An uncomplicated comparison between web log time stamps and authentication service logs would make it relatively simple to tie specific log-ins, queries, and downloads to specific individuals. In some instances, this log triangulation might even be applied to local users that gain access to services from a fixed IP address. Libraries should be very aware of the log-retention policies of their licensed resources, as well as those of their local web server managers.

Online Reference Transactions

Several libraries now offer some sort of online reference service, whether via e-mail, online chat, or more sophisticated co-browsing software. Libraries that offer such services cannot do so, however, without a very specific statement about confidentiality, on the part of both the library and any vendor that might supply software or databases for the transactions. Public institutions that are subject to disclosure of e-mail correspondence should be careful to delete both stored queries and the corresponding replies that go to most e-mail programs' "sent" folders. Privacy concerns quickly become confidentiality concerns when the nature of research is sensitive enough to affect livelihood, reputation, and just compensation for good ideas. Internet search engines are notorious for capturing visitor IPs, data on number and length of visits, and search queries. This same data, when retained by libraries, would amount to a major infringement of confidentiality. Imagine patent and trademark queries obtained by a third party, either through normal channels or by way of illegal (yet readily available) sniffer programs (network sniffers are hardware and software devices that can analyze data packets as they travel over networks).

Carefully crafted confidentiality agreements—something akin to doctor-patient, lawyer-client, or priest-parishioner relationships—might go a long way to ensuring libraries' victory over corporate for-profit research services. Will answers.google.com treat its queries with the same respect and confidentiality which libraries apply? It's quite amazing that in response to corporate competition for traditional library markets, libraries have not made a bigger deal of this major distinction between their services and those provided by entities with no particular ethical obligations.

MyLibrary

Attempts have already been made to write the history of the Internet, based on the assumption that its rapid growth and importance make even its short life span worthy of a history. When future histories are written, some will undoubtedly describe the late 1990s and early twenty-first century as the I-me-mine phase of Internet service. From MyYahoo to MySchwab, the personalization and customization features on the Web offer seemingly endless opportunities to create one personalized storefront after another. Even this author's employer joined the fray early with its open source MyLibrary@ NCState software, which is designed to combat information glut while offering customizable interfaces to data based on the patron's declared subject area. Other library portals soon followed at Cornell, the University of Washington, Virginia Commonwealth University, the University of Toronto, and many others. While the features, challenges, and opportunities of library portals are too numerous to either summarize or debate here, they do represent an important departure that is worth mentioning in light of this chapter's focus.

Library portals tie users to data; they generate logs of use, queries, research topics, personal preferences, and even personal information. This departure provides real service to users who want personalized access to library resources, but it also puts information about users in one place and stores information about them that libraries do not usually handle. Perhaps the next generation of library portals will address this privacy and confidentiality issue in more depth and determine if the convenience is worth the data collected about their users.

FROM PRIVACY POLICE TO PRIVACY AMBASSADORS

The goal in this section is not to tear down successful digital library services; on the contrary, some of these features are extremely useful, and the success of libraries in the information economy is directly tied to them. But this does not mean that libraries can blame technological advances for ethical attrition. Privacy is still a cornerstone of the profession, and as such, deserves stalwart attention and concern. As libraries apply that attention, they may find themselves reclaiming the ethical bond they have traditionally maintained with patrons, or they may choose to adapt carefully to lower patron expectations.

Who would guess that the U.S. Department of Commerce would create a list of principles outlining the importance of informational privacy? Nevertheless, the government agency has listed seven basic guidelines for measuring, applying, and ensuring informational privacy rights.[4] Libraries might use this same list to measure the adequacy of those with whom they transact business for online information.

> *Notice:* An organization collecting personal data must inform the individuals involved of what they are doing and their rights.
>
> *Choice:* Individuals must be able to opt out of their data being transmitted to third parties.
>
> *Onward transmission:* Personal data can only be transmitted to third parties that subscribe to privacy protection.
>
> *Security:* Organizations collecting personal data must hold them secure against misuse, disclosure, destruction, and so on.
>
> *Data integrity:* Personal data may only be used for the purposes for which they were collected.

Access: Individuals must have reasonable access to the data that have been collected about them.

Enforcement: There must be mechanisms (governmental or private) to ensure compliance with privacy principles. Those mechanisms must include recourse for individuals whose data have been misused, follow-up procedures to ensure remedies are being applied, and sanctions against organizations that violate personal privacy rights.

Libraries face a significant challenge in testing these criteria against the myriad of privacy statements, terms of use, and personal data storage policies offered (or not) by numerous online vendors, especially the ones that libraries know their patrons are using. An exciting development from the W3C, the governing body of the World Wide Web, could mitigate this difficult task. The Platform for Privacy Preferences, or P3P, would compare a user's privacy profile with the standard privacy disclosure of the visited website. P3Ps that do not match the preferences on the website would warn the user about possible privacy infringement. Extended to the information profession, libraries could conceivably rate the privacy adherence of various online content providers, or use such data in making determinations about license agreements, renewals, or collection development policies. While critics feel that there might not be enough incentive for websites to offer a standardized form of privacy information, the vendors that libraries deal with may have more incentive if prompted by the largest customer base with the most concern for privacy on the Internet. Despite efforts such as P3P, however, the standard has no teeth without an enforcement provision like the one in the list of privacy principles from the Commerce Department.

Adapting to Lower Expectations, or Not

This chapter is not meant to be overly critical of librarians; in fact, while consumer advocates enjoy most of the media spotlight on privacy and confidentiality issues, the professional literature and opinion belong mostly to information professionals. On the other hand, one can hope that a more critical approach to online services in libraries will uncover the potential pitfalls of privacy concerns.

Over the next five to ten years, libraries will undoubtedly be adapting their practices to match the personal conveniences offered by several online companies. They must do so, however, without acquiescing to the wholesale forfeiture of confidentiality and privacy for the sake of convenience, effi-ciency, and cost concerns. Careful marketing of the same personalization and customization services provided by online vendors, and anonymous or confi-dential brokering of other services, will provide some middle ground that provides service to the user while continuing to distinguish libraries from their corporate counterparts. The use of the business model planning, out-lined in chapter 4, will also help inform libraries about which services mean the most to their patrons and offer a return on investment over return on per-sonal data.

The horrific events of September 11, and the aftermath of the govern-ment's efforts to ensure homeland security, have breathed new life into the debates over patron privacy (and several other debates concerning access to information). These debates are quite possibly more divisive than they have ever been in the history of libraries. The impact of legal changes in the wake of the terrorist attacks is yet to be determined, and is beyond the scope of this book; nevertheless, libraries should welcome debate on one of the corner-stones of the profession, and take the opportunity to both reevaluate old prac-tices and determine the privacy concerns surrounding new ones. Distinct and well-articulated policies of privacy, anonymity, and confidentiality will go a long way to establishing, or reestablishing, the relationship of trust that exists between libraries and their patrons, and which sets libraries apart from their vendor and dot-com counterparts. The biggest debate over information pri-vacy in the twenty-first century will likely center around who poses a larger threat to the consumer, governments or corporations. Either way, libraries stand poised to be privacy's greatest defenders.

Notes

The second epigraph for this chapter is from Josh Dubeuman and Michael Beaudet, "Privacy Perspectives for Online Searchers: Confidentiality with Confidence?" *Searcher* 8, no. 7 (2000): 32.

1. Michael Gorman, "Privacy," in *Our Enduring Values: Librarianship in the Twenty-First Century* (Chicago: American Library Association, 2000), 144.
2. Janet L. Balas, "How Should Privacy Be Protected in the Electronic Library," *Computers in Libraries* 21, no. 6 (2001): 55.
3. American Library Association, "Q&A on the Confidentiality and Privacy of Library Records," *Newsletter on Intellectual Freedom* 50, no. 6 (2001): 240.
4. Quoted in Gorman, "Privacy," 150.

8 | RADICAL NOTIONS AND CONCLUSIONS

Can libraries flourish in an information economy at the speed of the Internet? Can anyone glean calm recommendations from the seemingly frenzied state of affairs in the information industry? This author sincerely hopes that the radical notions put forth in this book will be the clichéd responses of tomorrow's informed, technically savvy, and business-minded cadre of librarians. That hope aside, this final chapter offers some concluding reflections and summary.

INFORMATION EXPERTISE

"The question of who is to do library automation—librarians or computer experts—is no longer meaningful."[1] Richard De Gennaro came to this conclusion almost thirty-five years ago; perhaps it is time to alter it a bit and say that the question of who is to do information automation—librarians, their vendors, or dot-com entrepreneurs—is no longer meaningful. Recognition that all three are doing it, however, *is* meaningful. Like it or not, the developmental and programming muscle still belongs to library vendors and Internet companies. How (or whether) libraries will affect that development is up to both parties, but must begin with libraries. If libraries are to contribute their own programming muscle to information technology, they should do so as complements to digital library services, or as solutions to service failings, not purely out of spite for an information industry that has traditionally controlled technology solutions.

This book has not intended to place library vendors and dot-coms in the same category; in fact, it has intended to more closely ally the priorities and strategies of libraries and their vendors. Both would do well to pay more attention to their dot-com counterparts. While they share many attributes, the fixed nature of library automation vendors' customer base should distinguish them from their dot-com counterparts. As such, library vendors have a unique interest in the professional development, technological expertise, and philosophical considerations of a vocal customer base. There are several ways in which both sides can capitalize on the codependent nature of their relationship.

Library-vendor exchange programs are just one radical notion on this front. Many libraries would gladly send their professionals to library vendors in order to teach the latter a thing or two about how libraries want to do business. The librarians themselves would likely come away with fresh insight into the perspective of a fast-paced industry that ultimately aims to please its customers (or its stockholders, as the case may be). On the flip side, libraries might leverage the programming or product management skills of library vendor development staff in return for sending librarians into the field. These borrowed skills could either be used for programming that is unique to the library's needs, or could involve modifications to software supplied by the vendor in question. The library gets unfettered access to professional programming and development skills, and the vendor gains insight into the needs of the library.

Library educators might consider a more systematic approach to preparing students to enter careers in the library vendor field. Certain vendors might even consider subsidizing such educational efforts in return for contractual work obligations by students upon graduation—sort of a library vendor ROTC program. In this way, library vendors gain access to the all-important formative stages of library education, and the library profession sends its own into the vendor field with the profession's interests at heart.

Less radical approaches, like formal library-vendor partnerships, codevelopment of library service products, and professional organization membership opportunities can also do their part to bring the library and vendor communities closer together. No longer two separate camps, they have the potential to become two sides of the same coin, leveraged to take library automation forward in this century.

VALLEYS, PLATEAUS, AND MOUNTAINS

Nevertheless, there are those who might argue that libraries will not be able to climb their way out of the valley of tradition, culture, and status quo. Still others might argue (among them even library vendors themselves) that library automation has reached a plateau of functionality, leaving both vendors and libraries wondering what else there is to do in the industry—both in developing and delivering information. In fact, this notion poses a danger to library interests because it is only a matter of time before library automation vendors seek ways off their plateau. So far, vendors have merged with other vendors, gone out of business entirely, or expanded into new areas like network services or nonlibrary automation projects. None of these is necessarily in the best interest of libraries. This book suggests several areas into which libraries and vendors could expand their market cooperatively. Doing so has the potential to create revenue for library vendors, while continuing to ensure the mutually beneficial relationships with libraries that have existed for decades. Both parties need to foster the relationship if it is to continue in the future. Whether in the valley, or on the plateau, libraries and vendors must meet together to face the next mountain. Perhaps the information tools and commodities offered by Internet businesses are the next challenge for both.

When these challenges are not faced in concert, both camps face the danger of technology becoming an end in and of itself, rather than a means to an end. Without clearly defined challenges and concerns, libraries and vendors will both bury themselves in the minutia of technological concerns that no longer solve known problems. Paying attention to the business models of new Internet companies and information brokers, however, may shed new light on online services, desired functionality, and new frontiers of information delivery.

Despite partnership efforts, libraries will want to keep a collective eye on the plateau of library automation. As fewer but larger companies compete for a shrinking market space of new-name sales, the library vendor marketplace, especially for ILS companies, is bound to get interesting in the next decade. Some vendors will continue to concentrate on providing technology to customers whom they entrust with the responsibility for content. Others will seek the full integration between catalog and content, wedding two components that some libraries will continually strive to keep separated, for better or worse. This strategy certainly poses concerns for libraries that have already recognized the ineffective, and even dangerous, nature of products like Questia that force users into a tightly controlled world of information that excludes all other sources. Nevertheless, libraries need to find better ways to integrate online discovery with online delivery, or the disintermediated model will win the day, as users (and libraries) choose unmediated convenience over guided chaos.

Libraries should also be wary of the new library automation entrepreneur who attempts to pick up the slack from existing library vendors; this business model is especially prevalent in the open source community. Stopgap measures and quick fixes endanger libraries by returning to the days of modular systems that the next generation of librarians will struggle to integrate with existing systems and business models. Moreover, egocentric and single-developer products are dangerous bets when a library has limited technical support. Some library vendors, especially ILS companies, are already helping on this front by marketing some of these new technologies themselves, rather than attempting to build their own integrated versions of the same. This attempt at system integration is often an afterthought for the new library service entrepreneur, rather than a goal at the outset.

Finally, other ILS vendors will likely seek to repurpose existing software modules for new customers just waking up to the value of well-organized information. Digital information management systems—the catalogs of the twenty-first century—will bring new customers and new revenue to ILS vendors seeking to subsidize the relatively low prices that they charge to libraries. The danger for libraries here is marginalization by the very industry that it created and nurtured over the last four decades. An early and active role in this development strategy will place libraries at the forefront of library IT development.

TIMING, PACE, AND BUSINESS MODEL PLANNING

Libraries can continue to learn from their corporate counterparts when it comes to creating, delivering, and supporting digital library services. Three simple strategies will help libraries compete with and emulate successful business practices.

First, libraries must learn to look for expertise in the right places, and hire IT professionals with the same celerity with which they can acquire jobs in the private sector. There is a joke in library information technology that says the way to pay IT professionals what you can afford is to require an M.L.S. degree. Based in fact, this humorous truism not only shows that libraries need more IT expertise in their ranks, but also suggests a willingness among librarians to gain expertise that would be better compensated in the private sector.

The sooner libraries and information professionals work to shrink the distinctions between private and librarian sector information jobs, the better off everyone in the industry will be. As for the issue of speed in hiring, IT professionals, especially programmers, remain in heavy demand, despite the demise of several Internet ventures. When libraries have the chance to acquire them, they should take it; when library schools have the opportunity to train them for the information profession, they should jump at it.

Second, libraries need to move forward in embracing new technologies. They have already evolved from negative reactions to cautious approaches and then to reluctant adoption. In an information economy with corporate players, libraries must seek to embrace technological advances only slightly behind the curve, at worst, and well ahead of it, at best. Moreover, libraries should continue to emulate—and when necessary, attack—Internet business models that challenge *effective* library services that already exist. Petty jealousies and concerns over being misunderstood will not woo back customers. Creating viable and effective services that stand as alternatives to Internet counterparts keeps patrons and wins new ones.

Third, libraries must adapt to business models that foster the creation, maintenance, and product relevance of digital services. Effective evaluation of services, in conjunction with analysis of the value balance equation (see chapter 4), will help libraries develop strategic plans, form marketing strategies, and allow libraries to compete with (and defeat) Internet business alternatives.

DISTINGUISHING LIBRARIES IN THE INFORMATION INDUSTRY

The best part of all this is that not only can libraries accomplish these goals without sacrificing their professional and ethical integrity, they can do so while vindicating themselves at the same time. Libraries have the distinct advantage of ultimately being able to ignore the bottom line. Library service models that leverage the best of what is available on the Internet will fill the vacuum that failed Internet business models (based on those library service models) create when they go belly-up. Contentville and netLibrary are just two major examples of business models that could not make it; others are sure to follow. It is right and good that libraries continue to create and maintain the valuable business models that traditional businesses themselves cannot afford. When it comes to repackaging the materials that libraries provide better, it is the strong opinion of this author that most of these ventures will fail. It will be surprising if Questia is still around by the time this book is published. It is not that information wants to be free; librarians want information to be valuable, and this is where libraries come in, by adding the value of subject expertise, collection, and organization. Search, retrieval, delivery, and personalization are still distinct challenges, but ones that libraries can easily overcome by leveraging the expertise of corporate entities. Those same entities will likely never have the value sets—both professional value and ethical value—that libraries bring to the table.

But before librarians dance on the fresh graves of failed Internet business models, they must ensure that their own services include the applicable bells and whistles that will lure back, or capture for the first time, the online customer base that is now accustomed to a higher level of Internet service. Moreover, libraries should not take a reactive stance in capitalizing on the demise of Internet businesses, but should be positing themselves as viable alternatives in the present. When the rest fail, libraries will be there to pick up the ball.

Not only will libraries be there, they will stand ready with a suite of benefits that users of corporate sector services never cared about—preservation, standards, privacy, human contact, and value. Libraries will reintermediate themselves into information brokering (both automated and not) with the added values that some patrons expect from libraries and that others have forgotten ever existed. One can hope that libraries' traditional vendors will be there with them, helping them, offering the needed technology, distinct from content, and delivering content that is free from restrictive licensing and monopolistic prices. Even strange bedfellows can dream.

Note

1. Richard De Gennaro, "The Development and Administration of Automated Systems in Academic Libraries," *Journal of Library Automation* 1, no. 1 (1968): 80.

INTERNET COMPANIES, LIBRARY AUTOMATION VENDORS, AND INFORMATION ORGANIZATIONS

This book mentions several dot-coms, library vendors, and organizations with a stake in the library industry. This appendix is an effort to describe the general business and focus of each of these organizations. Without exception, the text of the descriptions is taken from the websites of these organizations. Very little editing has been applied to this text, so the reader should take superlatives, promises, and tales of greatness with a large grain of salt.

ADOBE

Founded in 1982, Adobe Systems, Inc., builds award-winning software solutions for network publishing, including web, print, video, wireless, and broadband applications. Its graphic design, imaging, dynamic media, and authoring tools enable customers to create, publish, and deliver visually rich content for various types of media. Adobe is the second largest PC software company in the United States, with annual revenues exceeding $1.2 billion. It employs over 2,800 employees worldwide.

ASK JEEVES

Ask Jeeves, Inc., is a leading provider of natural language, question-answering, and search technologies for consumers and companies. The company offers these technologies through two business units: Web Properties, a set of online media properties and search services; and Jeeves Solutions, an enterprise software business. Ask Jeeves Web Properties operates leading websites that provide consumers with a simple and fast way to find relevant answers to their questions. Ask Jeeves also syndicates its advance search technologies to web portals and content and destination sites to help companies increase user loyalty while generating revenue. Ask Jeeves Web Properties includes Ask.com, Ask.co.uk, Teoma.com, and Ask Jeeves for Kids.

CLIO

Clio is the most widely used interlibrary lending management system available today. More than 800 institutions have purchased Clio based upon recommendations from other ILL professionals and workshops on improving ILL operations. Clio is used in 48 U.S. states, the District of Columbia, Canada, Hong Kong, Australia, England, Scotland, and Wales. Clio is a complete ILL management system for the new world of information.

DIGITAL LIBRARY FEDERATION

The Digital Library Federation (DLF) is a consortium of libraries and related agencies that are pioneering in the use of electronic-information technologies to extend their collections and services. Through its members, the DLF provides leadership for libraries by identifying standards and "best practices" for digital collections and network access; coordinating leading-edge research and development in libraries' use of electronic-information technology; and helping start projects and services that libraries need but cannot develop individually. The DLF operates under the administrative umbrella of the Council of Library and Information Resources.

DIGITALOWL

DigitalOwl provides information-management application services that leverage digital rights management to solve critical business problems. Its products and services enable customers to securely license, promote, distribute, and manage premium information within end-user communities. Focused on secure information movement in financial, health care, publishing, and corporate markets, DigitalOwl understands the information issues facing these companies today and how to solve them effectively.

DOCUTEK

Docutek Information Systems is an Internet company that specializes in developing products and services for the educational market. It was one of the first companies to develop a web-based electronic reserve system, ERes, and web-enables a host of other library services through Docutek onCampus. ERes is the worldwide electronic reserves leader—nearly two million students at over 200 institutions spanning three continents have access to its services. Docutek strives to develop cutting-edge, cost-effective solutions that enhance the educational experience and enable academic institutions to better serve their students and faculty.

EBRARY

Ebrary is a leading provider of information distribution and retrieval services. The company's customizable ebrarian solution combines powerful software with copyright-protected books, journals, periodicals, and other online documents provided by more than 100 of the world's leading publishers. The ebrarian solution enables libraries, institutions, and other organizations to give their users access to high-value, authoritative materials and research tools that allow them to interact with content at the word level. Ebrary's publishing partners benefit from new sales and marketing opportunities on the Internet. Ebrary is privately held and is funded by Random House Ventures LLC, Pearson PLC, and the McGraw-Hill Companies.

EGAIN

EGain is a leading provider of eService software for the Internet, helping businesses transform their traditional call centers into multichannel eService networks. EGain's solutions for e-mail management, interactive web collaboration, intelligent self-help agents, knowledge management, and proactive online marketing can measurably improve operational efficiency and customer retention—resulting in significant return on investment.

ELIBRARY

ELibrary is a comprehensive digital archive for information seekers of all ages. Users can do business research, use it for homework, get background materials for term papers, find out about both current and historical events, and more, all in one vast database designed for both depth of content and simplicity of interface. Subscribers can ask questions in plain English, and eLibrary searches a billion words and thousands of images and quickly returns the information requested. With its one-stop research access, eLibrary aggregates hundreds and hundreds of full-text periodicals, nine international newswires, classic books, hundreds of maps, and thousands of photographs, as well as major works of literature, art, and reference.

ENDEAVOR INFORMATION SYSTEMS

Endeavor Information Systems, Inc., has been providing integrated library management systems since its inception in 1994. With an executive team base that has a strong heritage in the library industry, Endeavor grounds its product line development in knowledge, commitment, and the embrace of proven new technologies. The first Voyager ILS was sold to Michigan Technological University, and Endeavor's momentum has continued since that time. With library customers of all sizes and a commitment to forward-thinking product development, Endeavor Information Systems is poised for the future of library collection management.

EPIXTECH

With more than 7,000 customer libraries, epixtech is the leader in installed library systems and serves public, academic, special, and school libraries around the world. Epixtech, Inc., was formed in December 1999 by the private investment purchase of Ameritech Library Services from SBC Ameritech. Ameritech Library Services had been formed by the merger of Dynix and NOTIS Systems, Inc.—two premier library systems providers. Epixtech continues to lead the industry as the largest library systems provider in the world, with more than twenty years of experience.

EX LIBRIS

The Ex Libris group is a worldwide supplier of software solutions and related services for libraries and information centers. The company's flagship product, ALEPH 500, is a market leader in the field of library automation for higher education as well as for public, national, and research libraries, consortia and national networks, and large corporations. Based in Israel, Ex Libris has five fully owned subsidiaries—in the United States, the United Kingdom, Germany, Australia, and Luxembourg. Its staff consists of 193 employees worldwide (as of September 2001), with a core development team that includes both highly qualified librarians and expert software engineers. Local offices and distributors provide sales, project management, and support operations. In addition, the company offers analysis, data conversion, project management, and training services as part of its policy to tailor the solution to the specific institution and to help local staff learn how to use the system to its fullest capabilities.

EZPROXY (FROM USEFUL UTILITIES)

EZproxy is an easy-to-set-up and easy-to-maintain program for providing your users with remote access to web-based licensed databases. It is available for servers running Linux, Solaris, or Windows NT. It operates as an intermediary server between your users and your licensed databases. Your users connect to EZproxy, then it connects on their behalf to your licensed databases to obtain web pages and send them back to your users. The result is a seamless access environment for your users without the need for automatic proxy configuration files. EZproxy only alters references to your database vendor's web pages, so if your database vendor provides additional links to other free web pages on the Internet, these are left as is. In this manner, if your users elect to follow one of these links, the EZproxy server is automatically taken out of the communication loop.

GEMSTAR

Gemstar eBook Group, Ltd., focuses on developing state-of-the-art technology for dedicated reading devices and provides reading content for these devices. Gemstar eBook Group is a subsidiary of Gemstar TV Guide.

ILLIAD (FROM OCLC)

The OCLC ILLiad resource-sharing management software automates routine interlibrary loan functions so you can provide faster service in a modern, paper-free environment. Library staff save time by managing all of their library's borrowing, lending, and document delivery through a single Windows-based interface. Library users can easily send and track their requests electronically through the Web. OCLC ILLiad automatically processes filled requests and contacts users when requests are completed.

INFOTRIEVE

Infotrieve, Inc., is the definitive research portal, leading the market in article research and delivery. Its mission is to facilitate efficient, affordable, and innovative methods of distributing published materials to end-users, while protecting the rights of the information provider. To fulfill this mission, Infotrieve creates a one-stop shopping source, offering end-to-end capabilities for library and research needs. Combining high responsiveness with cost efficiency, the extensive Infotrieve network provides access to the world's largest library of journal content, exemplified by its breakthrough system, Virtual Library. Vast information and journalistic resources are available with varied choices in distribution, namely aggregated electronic and paper delivery, a distinct advantage over paper-only aggregation.

INNOVATIVE INTERFACES

Innovative Interfaces, Inc., was founded in 1978 and promptly made history with the first "black box" for libraries—a highly successful online interface that allowed libraries to download bibliographic data from OCLC to a local circulation system in real time, without rekeying. More than twenty years later, Innovative is still making history and setting the standard for excellence in library automation. Innovative is privately owned and exclusively involved with library automation and libraries. Thus, the company is totally focused on delivery and support of best-in-class software and services.

JSTOR

Originally conceived by William G. Bowen, president of the Andrew W. Mellon Foundation, JSTOR began as an effort to ease the increasing problems faced by libraries seeking to provide adequate stack space for long runs of back files of scholarly journals. In the broadest sense, JSTOR's mission is to help the scholarly community take advantage of advances in information technologies. In pursuing this mission, JSTOR has adopted a system-wide perspective, taking into account the sometimes conflicting needs of libraries, publishers, and scholars. JSTOR's goals include the following: to build a reliable and comprehensive archive of important scholarly journal literature; to dramatically improve access to these journals; to help fill gaps in existing library collections of journal back files; to address preservation issues such as mutilated pages and long-term deterioration of paper copy; to reduce the long-term capital and operating costs of libraries associated with the storage and care of journal collections; to assist scholarly associations and publishers in making the transition to electronic modes of publication; and to study the impact of providing electronic access on the use of these scholarly materials.

KANA

Founded in 1996, KANA provides the industry's leading external-facing eCRM solutions to the largest businesses in the world, helping them to better service, market to, and understand their customers and partners, while improving results and decreasing costs in contact centers and marketing departments. Through comprehensive, multichannel customer-relationship management that combines the best-in-class KANA iCARE architecture with enterprise applications, KANA has become the fastest-growing provider of next-generation eCRM technology. The company's customer-focused service, marketing, and commerce software applications enable organizations to improve customer and partner relationships by enabling them to productively interact when, where, and how they want—across all touch points, including web contact, web collaboration, e-mail, and telephone. KANA has twenty-two locations worldwide.

LIBRARYHQ.COM

LibraryHQ.com hosts varied resources and services for the wired librarian, including SiteSource, a subscription service of cataloged websites; MARCit, a downloadable source for electronic resource cataloging records; SiteServices, web customization services; and iKnow, a web-based catalog interface.

LIVEPERSON

LivePerson is a provider of online sales and customer service solutions. Over 2,500 websites currently use LivePerson solutions to answer customer questions, satisfy customers, build relationships, and deliver results. LivePerson Exchange enables operators to interact online with their customers at critical moments during their visit. LivePerson offers websites a timely and cost-effective means of providing customers with a number of options to communicate with them online. Combining the interactive nature of the Internet with the dependability of traditional customer service, LivePerson can help you build strong and lasting relationships, convert browsers into buyers, and turn one-time visitors into loyal customers.

LIZARDTECH

LizardTech develops imaging software and solutions that simplify and enhance the distribution, management, and control of digital images and documents. LizardTech is focused on innovative solutions that provide users of all levels with bandwidth optimization and instant access to high-resolution, multipurpose digital images and multimedia content.

LUNA IMAGING

Luna Imaging, Inc., makes it easier than ever to build comprehensive digital image collections by offering state-of-the-art image management software, Insight, along with a variety of ways to quickly and easily build your collections. Collection managers can digitize their own image collections and incorporate them into Luna's Insight software, share content with other institutions that use Insight, subscribe to digital image collections through a variety of Luna's content partners, or license digital images from the growing number of Insight-ready image collections now available.

MUSEGLOBAL

Muse delivers a one-stop integrated search environment offering better, more effective ways to aggregate, disseminate, and deliver real-time information for individual libraries and groups of libraries. Muse offers expanded information services to patrons, such as customized interfaces for member organizations, "branded" delivery of information, optimized and refined delivery of results, and consistency. Muse provides broadcast searching of web, Z39.50, SQL, and proprietary data sources simultaneously. Muse's Just in Time Enrichment service enhances bibliographic record display so that information such as tables of contents, book reviews, and jacket art can be added in real time to record results.

NETLIBRARY (FROM OCLC)

Founded in August 1998, netLibrary is one of the world's leading providers of electronic books and helps academic, public, corporate, and special libraries create a richer, more productive learning environment for their patrons. By combining the time-honored traditions of the library system with electronic publishing, netLibrary offers an easy-to-use information and retrieval system for accessing the full text of reference, scholarly, and professional books. NetLibrary is a division of the Online Computer Library Center (OCLC), a nonprofit organization that provides computer-based cataloging, reference, resource-sharing, and preservation services to libraries worldwide.

NISO (NATIONAL INFORMATION STANDARDS ORGANIZATION)

NISO, a nonprofit association accredited by the American National Standards Institute, identifies, develops, maintains, and publishes technical standards to manage information in our changing and ever more digital environment.

NISO standards apply both traditional and new technologies to the full range of information-related needs, including retrieval, repurposing, storage, metadata, and preservation. NISO was founded in 1939, incorporated as a not-for-profit education association in 1983, and assumed its current name the following year. NISO draws its support from the communities it serves. The leaders of more than seventy organizations in the fields of publishing, libraries, information technology, and media serve as its voting members. Hundreds of experts and practitioners serve on NISO committees and as officers of the association.

NIST (NATIONAL INSTITUTE OF STANDARDS AND TECHNOLOGY)

From automated teller machines and atomic clocks to mammograms and semiconductors, innumerable products and services rely in some way on the technology, measurements, and standards provided by the National Institute of Standards and Technology. Founded in 1901, NIST is a nonregulatory federal agency within the U.S. Commerce Department's Technology Administration. NIST's mission is to develop and promote measurements, standards, and technology to enhance productivity, facilitate trade, and improve the quality of life.

NORTHERN LIGHT

Northern Light uses patented classification intelligence and precision relevancy ranking to deliver accurate, relevant results from its special collection of more than 7,100 respected full-text publications, which are organized into "custom search folders" so that users don't have to waste time weeding through useless information. Enterprise clients can also search an index of more than 350 million web pages. With Northern Light's SinglePoint custom content-integration service, customers can even search their licensed third-party content and internal content, all with a single query, classified to a uniform standard and relevance ranked, thus using all the information available to them in one simple operation.

OCLC (ONLINE COMPUTER LIBRARY CENTER)

Founded in 1967 by university presidents to share library resources and reduce library costs, OCLC is a nonprofit membership organization serving 41,000 libraries in 82 countries and territories around the world. Its mission is to further access to the world's information and reduce library costs by offering services for libraries and their users. OCLC will be the leading global library cooperative, helping libraries serve people by providing economical access to knowledge through innovation and collaboration.

QUESTIA

Questia is the first online library that provides 24/7 access to the world's largest online collection of books and journal articles in the humanities and social sciences. You can search each and every word of all of the books and journal articles in the collection. You can read every title cover to cover. This rich, scholarly content—selected by professional collection development librarians—is not available elsewhere on the Internet. Undergraduates, high schoolers, graduate students, and Internet users of all ages have found Questia to be an invaluable online resource. Anyone doing research or just interested in topics that touch on the humanities and social sciences will find titles of interest in Questia.

REED ELSEVIER

Reed Elsevier is a world-leading publisher and information provider, operating in four core segments: Science and Medical, Legal, Education, and Business. Its principal activities are in North America and Europe and the company employs approximately 37,000 people. Reed Elsevier's key objective is to be the indispensable source of information-driven services and solutions to its target customers through the delivery of highly valued and demonstrably superior and flexible solutions, increasingly via the Internet.

SIRSI

The Sirsi Corporation recognizes that libraries today are on a mission to break down walls—barriers that limit the information and resources accessible to library users. A partner with academic, public, school, government, and special libraries, as well as consortia, Sirsi delivers software and services that assist libraries in expanding the diversity of their user communities and enhancing the library experience of those users. At Sirsi, our more than twenty-five years in the business have been focused on providing software and services that help libraries of all types and sizes serve their user communities. And since the merger with Data Research Associates (DRA), Sirsi has even more to offer, from e-library, integrated library management, and digital archiving solutions to a comprehensive slate of library technology services.

SWETS BLACKWELL

Swets Blackwell provides numerous options for academic, medical, corporate and government libraries and information centers worldwide. Its range of information and serials management services assist in optimizing resources in today's dynamic and increasingly complex electronic environment. Acting as an intermediary between libraries and information centers, Swets Blackwell works with publishers to provide customers with services for all types of serials.

SPARC (SCHOLARLY PUBLISHING AND ACADEMIC RESOURCES COALITION)

SPARC is an alliance of universities, research libraries, and organizations that was founded as a constructive response to market dysfunctions in the scholarly communication system. These dysfunctions have reduced the dissemination of scholarship and crippled libraries. SPARC serves as a catalyst for action, helping to create systems that expand information dissemination and use in a networked digital environment while responding to the needs of scholars and academia. SPARC's agenda focuses on enhancing broad and cost-effective access to peer-reviewed scholarship.

SYNDETIC SOLUTIONS

Syndetic Solutions is a provider of specialized bibliographic data to producers of electronic databases in the retail book trade, and a developer of custom thesauri, indexes, and vocabulary analysis and processing services for database producers, Internet search engines, and Internet directory services.

TDNET

TDNet's unique solution to electronic journals management is based on an original approach integrating a diversity of access modes to electronic journals on one unified, coherent site. TDNet is a custom-made e-journal service, tailored to include all and only a library's chosen titles, and to reflect the library's current access arrangements for every title on the system. TDNet's database currently holds over 28,000 e-journal websites and table of contents records for over 25,000 titles. Requests for titles which have not yet been added to TDNet's fast-growing database are welcome. TDNet's team constantly browses the web for more titles. TDNet is a perfect solution for academic, medical, corporate, and government organizations.

TLC (THE LIBRARY CORPORATION)

TLC evolved from providing MARCFICHE to more than 5,000 libraries in the 1970s and 1980s. TLC's ability to provide needed solutions to the library world and its place in the library marketplace were strengthened by the company's June 2000 acquisition of the CARL Corporation, a developer of technological solutions used by the largest public libraries in the United States and across the world. TLC's groundbreaking products include the pioneering cataloging system BiblioFile and the powerful automation systems Library. Solution and CARL.Solution. Both are used in libraries of all sizes throughout the world.

24/7

24/7 Reference is a set of software tools that enables librarians to provide real-time reference assistance to their patrons over the Internet. Each library can customize these tools to best serve its community.

VIRTUAL REFERENCE DESK (FROM LSSI)

The Virtual Reference Desk is a suite of products and services specifically designed to make web reference service easy, quick, and cost-effective for libraries. The backbone of LSSI's Virtual Reference Desk is the web collaboration software . . . sometimes also called Web Contact Center Software. LSSI has taken the same web collaboration software used so effectively by Webhelp and other major e-commerce sites and adapted it for use by libraries.

VTLS

VTLS, Inc., is an international market leader in the development of solutions for library automation, resource-sharing networks and digital libraries. These solutions, Virtua ILS (Integrated Library Systems), Visual MIS (Multimedia and Imaging Solutions), and Vista CPS (Companion Product Suite), easily work in tandem or apart. During the past thirteen years, more than 900 libraries have chosen VTLS's software and services as the superior solution for their collections. Customers include academic, public, corporate, and special libraries located throughout the United States, Canada, and thirty-two other countries.

WEBHELP

The ARENA eCRM Suite, comprising the next generation of online customer-relationship management products, has been built on years of extensive CRM and eCRM experience. It offers industry-leading technology solutions that enable businesses to provide online customer support in a quick and cost-effective manner. The integral part of Webhelp's ARENA eCRM technology platform is our proprietary Web Application Event Framework, an open standards-based "zero-latency" framework that enables "true" real-time online communication. Components that enable services such as live chat and e-mail communication can be independently added, modified, and combined to meet the specific needs of each client.

XANEDU

The keystone of XanEdu's success is a suite of unparalleled resources that empower faculty to create print and digital coursepacks. XanEdu's enormous collection of digital content, its fully customizable coursepack system, research tools, and copyright and expert developmental support offer everything needed to create the perfect resource to enhance the classroom—and virtual classroom—experience.

B | LIBRARY AUTOMATION VENDOR SURVEY

This survey is solely the creation of its author and is not in any way related to the activities of NC State University or the NCSU Libraries. Responses are voluntary. Responses will not be used to endorse one business product over another. Any extrapolations made from the survey for publication will be verified by the author with the applicable vendor before inclusion in any published work.

March 15, 2001

To Whom It May Concern:

My name is Andrew Pace, and I am a systems librarian at the North Carolina State University Libraries in Raleigh, N.C. I am also an author for the American Library Association. This year, I am working on the completion of two pieces for ALA Editions, and I respectfully ask that you take a look at the enclosed questions and consider responding soon so that I can include your company in my discussions.

The first piece, for *Library Technology Reports,* investigates optimizing library websites. Since so many of a library's offerings are integrated third-party products, your input in this area will be invaluable. The second, a book titled *Strange Bedfellows* [working title of *The Ultimate Digital Library*], looks at the cooperative (and sometime competitive) relationships between libraries, library automation vendors, and Internet companies.

Both of these works will endeavor to shed an honest light on the mutually enriching relationships between libraries and the information industry. None of the information gathered will be used to endorse the services of one company over another; receiving a response, however, will ensure your company's inclusion in discussions of these relationships.

Please do not hesitate to call or e-mail me if you have any questions about this survey. Please feel free to add any information that you think might be relevant to either discussion.

Regards,

Andrew K. Pace

VENDOR AUTOMATION SURVEY

Complete this form online at
    http://www.lib.ncsu.edu/systems/pace/vendorsurvey.html

(1) How long has your company had its own business web presence (i.e., your own website)? _____

    (1a) How many major design changes to your web presence have you undertaken in that time? _____

(2) How long has your company marketed web-based products and services? _____

    (2a) How many major design changes to your web-based products and services have you undertaken in that time? _____

(3) Is there a person or unit within your organization solely responsible for interface usability testing? _____

    (3a) Describe your usability testing procedures. _____

    _____

    _____

    _____

(4) Does your company have a forum for users (both individual and institutional) to submit feedback about your online products? If so, what is it? _____

    _____

    (4a) Do users take advantage of feedback opportunities? _____

    (4b) How is user feedback incorporated into your product development?_____

    _____

(5) What online product lines or strategies has your company abandoned entirely (e.g., plug-ins, SGML, DHTML, etc.)? Why? _____

    _____

    _____

    _____

(6) How many staff work for your organization? _____

   (6a) How many of your staff are professional librarians? _____

   (6b) What is the average number of years that those professionals have worked in a library? _____

   (6c) Does your company include librarians working for you in an advisory or consulting capacity? _____

(7) What strategies is your company using to address ADA requirements for people with disabilities (e.g., screen-readable interfaces, Bobby compliance, etc.)? _____

_____

_____

_____

   (7a) Would library feedback in this area be beneficial to your company? _____

(8) Describe your company's strategic vision for doing business in the information industry of the twenty-first century. _____

_____

_____

_____

_____

_____

Please furnish a name with contact information for possible follow-up.

Name: _____

E-mail: _____

Phone: _____

BIBLIOGRAPHY

Aiman-Smith, Lynda, and Mitzi Montoya-Weiss. "Application of Business Models to the Library: Service Portfolio Mapping." Raleigh, N.C., 2000.

Alfino, Mark. "Information Ethics in the Workplace." *Journal of Information Ethics* 10, no. 2 (2001): 5–8.

American Library Association. "Q&A on the Confidentiality and Privacy of Library Records." *Newsletter on Intellectual Freedom* 50, no. 6 (2001): 239–40.

Argentati, Carolyn. "Guidelines for Business Model Planning for Library Services." Raleigh: North Carolina State University Libraries (Draft Report), 2000.

Balas, Janet L. "How Should Privacy Be Protected in the Electronic Library." *Computers in Libraries* 21, no. 6 (2001): 53–55.

Berry, John. "Departing Shots from Richard De Gennaro." *Library Journal* 120, no. 19 (1995): 30–31.

Besser, Howard. "Commodification of Information and the Assault on Public Space." Presentation given at the I. T. Littleton Seminar, North Carolina State University Libraries, 2002.

Bogart, Dave, ed. *Bowker Annual: Library and Book Trade Almanac.* 46th ed. New Providence, N.J.: R. R. Bowker, 2001.

Bowen, William G. "At a Slight Angle to the Universe: The University in a Digitized, Commercialized Age." *ARL,* no. 216 (2001): 1–15.

Breeding, Marshall. "The Open Source ILS: Still Only a Distant Possibility." *Information Technology and Libraries* 21, no. 1 (2002): 16–18.

Bretthauer, David. "Open Source Software: A History." *Information Technology and Libraries* 21, no. 1 (2002): 3–10.

Casey, Robert S., et al., eds. *Punched Cards: The Applications to Science and Industry.* 2nd ed. New York: Reinhold Publishing, 1958.

Coffman, Steven. "Building the World's Largest Library: Driving the Future." *Searcher* 7, no. 3 (1999): 34–37.

———. "The Response to 'Building the World's Largest Library.'" *Searcher* 7, no. 7 (1999): 28–32.

Cox, N. S. M., J. D. Dews, and J. L. Dolby. *The Computer and the Library: The Role of the Computer in the Organization and Handling of Information in Libraries.* Newcastle upon Tyne, Eng.: University Library Publications, 1966.

Coyle, Karen. "Open Source, Open Standards." *Information Technology and Libraries* 21, no. 1 (2002): 33–36.

Creighton, Kim, and Bruce Jenson. "The Public Library of the Future." *Library Journal* 126, no. 13 (2001): 56–58.

Cronin, Blaise. "The Dreaded 'L' Word." *Library Journal* 126, no. 5 (2001): 58.

De Gennaro, Richard. "The Development and Administration of Automated Systems in Academic Libraries." *Journal of Library Automation* 1, no. 1 (1968): 75–91.

———. "Library Automation: Changing Patterns and New Directions." *Library Journal* 119, no. 17 (1994): 8–12.

Dewey, Barbara I. *Library User Education: Powerful Learning, Powerful Partnerships.* Lanham, Md.: Scarecrow, 2001.

Dorman, David. "Ebrary at Bat." *American Libraries* 33, no. 1 (2002): 96–97.

Dubeuman, Josh, and Michael Beaudet. "Privacy Perspectives for Online Searchers: Confidentiality with Confidence?" *Searcher* 8, no. 7 (2000): 32–48.

Dunn, Ron. "Internet Librarian Breakfast Session." Presentation given at the Internet Librarian Conference, Monterey, Calif., 1998.

Ehresmann, Julia, ed. *The Bowker Annual of Library and Book Trade Information.* 29th ed. New York: R. R. Bowker, 1984.

Feinberg, Renee. "B&N: The New College Library?" *Library Journal* 123, no. 3 (1998): 49–51.

————, ed. *The Changing Culture of Libraries.* Jefferson, N.C.: McFarland, 2001.

Fialkoff, Francine. "Flexing Market Muscle." *Library Journal* 123, no. 12 (1998): 73.

————. "Large Market, Small Voice." *Library Journal* 125, no. 20 (2000): 104.

————. "Where's the Library Model." *Library Journal* 125, no. 13 (2000): 78.

Gibbons, Susan. "Growing Competition for Libraries." *Library Hi Tech* 19, no. 4 (2001).

————. "Interview with Christopher Warnock, CEO, CTO and Co-Founder of ebrary." *Librarian's eBook Newsletter* 2, no. 4 (2002).

————. "Long-Awaited ebrary Has Arrived." *Librarian's eBook Newsletter* 2, no. 3 (2002).

Gorman, Michael. "Privacy." *In Our Enduring Values: Librarianship in the Twenty-First Century,* 144–57. Chicago: American Library Association, 2000.

Greenstein, Daniel, and Jerry George. "Building a Library Service Network." *CLIR Issues,* no. 23 (2001): 3–7.

Harris, Lesley Ellen. "Deal-Maker, Deal-Breaker: When to Walk Away." *Library Journal Netconnect* (2000): 12–14.

Head, Alison. "Web Redemption and the Promise of Usability." *Online* 23, no. 6 (1999): 20–23.

Helfer, Doris Small. "To Questia or Not to Questia, That Is the Question." *Searcher* 9, no. 4 (2001): 31–35.

Heller, Anne, and Elizabeth Lorenzen. "Online Ordering: Making Its Mark." *Library Journal* 124, no. 14 (1999): 153–58.

Herring, Mark Y. "Our Times, They Are a-Changin', But Are We?" *Library Journal* 126, no. 17 (2001): 42–44.

Hilts, Paul. "Ebrary Adds Research Service, Expands Access." *Publishers Weekly* 248, no. 20 (2001): 18.

————. "Ebrary.Com Offers Web as Serious Research Tool." *Publishers Weekly* 247, no. 13 (2000): 28.

Jascó, Péter. "They Didn't Come (in Droves)." *Information Today* 18, no. 10 (2001): 30–31.

KALIPER Advisory Committee. "Educating Library and Information Science Professionals for a New Century: The Kaliper Report." Reston: Association for Library and Information Science Education, 2000.

Klein, Joelle. "Duke Study: Users at Library for Net." *Library Journal* 123, no. 8 (1998): 14.

Lichtenberg, James. "What Can Publishers Learn from Librarians." *Publishers Weekly* 248, no. 12 (2001): 17.

Mandel, Charles. "Somebody Call the Library Cops." *Canadian Business* 73, no. 19 (2000): 27.

Matthews, Judy, and Richard W. Wiggins. "Scholarly Sources in a Googley World." *Library Journal* 126, no. 15 (2001): 35.

McDermott, Irene E. "Books in Print Wrestles with Amazon." *Searcher* 9, no. 7 (2001): 53–56.

McKiernan, Gerry. E-mail, August 2000.

Miller, Dick R. "XML: Libraries' Strategic Opportunity." *Library Journal Netconnect* (2000): 18–22.

Moran, Barbara B. "Practitioners vs. LIS Educators: Time to Reconnect." *Library Journal* 126, no. 18 (2001): 52–55.

Mount, Ellis, ed. *Opening New Doors: Alternative Careers for Librarians.* Washington, D.C.: Special Libraries Association, 1993.

Neuman, Delia. "The World Wide Web as a Tool for Information Retrieval: An Exploratory Study of Users' Strategies in an Open-Ended System." *School Library Media Quarterly* 25 (1997): 229–36.

Nielsen, Jakob. *Designing Web Usability.* Indianapolis: New Riders, 2000.

Oder, Norman. "Cataloging the Net: Two Years Later." *Library Journal* 125, no. 16 (2000): 50–51.

———. "Patriot Act and Privacy Concerns." *Library Journal* 127, no. 3 (2002): 16.

———. "Peter McCracken: Librarian as Entrepreneur." *Library Journal* 126, no. 13 (2001): 44–46.

———. "The Shape of E-Reference." *Library Journal* 126, no. 2 (2001): 46–49.

———. "2000 Grad Joel Summerlin: New Orders." *Library Journal* 126, no. 17 (2001): 38.

O'Leary, Mick. "Ebrary Shapes New Ebook Paradigm." *EContent* 24, no. 2 (2001): 58–59.

———. "Missing the Point on Contentville." *Information Today* 18, no. 3 (2001): 20–21.

———. "New Academic Information Model Bypasses Libraries." *Online* 25, no. 4 (2001): 72–74.

Ormsby, Eric. "The Battle of the Book: The Research Library Today." *New Criterion* (2001): 4–16.

Pace, Andrew K. "Optimizing Library Web Services: A Usability Approach." *Library Technology Reports* 38, no. 2 (2002): 1–81.

Pantry, Sheila, ed. *Your Successful LIS Career: Planning Your Career, CVs, Interviews, and Self Promotion.* London: Library Association Publishing, 1999.

Parker, Ralph H. *Library Applications of Punched Cards: A Description of Mechanical Systems.* Chicago: American Library Association, 1952.

————. "The Punched Card Method in Circulation Work." *Library Journal* 61 (1936): 903–5.

Rogers, Michael. "Ebrary Offers Digital Twist on Photocopying Model." *Library Journal* 125, no. 10 (2000): 27.

————. "Ebrary Releases Ebrarian 2.0 Enhanced Library Package." *Library Journal* 127, no. 2 (2002): 29.

Sellen, Betty-Carol, ed. *What Else Can You Do with a Library Degree.* New York: Neal-Schuman, 1997.

St. Lifer, Evan. "Tapping into the Zen of Marketing." *Library Journal* 126, no. 8 (2001): 44–46.

Tennant, Roy. "The Digital Library Divide." *Library Journal* 126, no. 13 (2001): 37–38.

Tenopir, Carol. "I Never Learned That in Library School." *Online* 24, no. 2 (2000): 43–46.

————. "Trends for the Next Five Years." *Library Journal* 125, no. 16 (2000): 38–39.

Terrell, Tom, and Vicki L. Gregory. "Plenty of Jobs, Salaries Flat." *Library Journal* 126, no. 17 (2001): 34–40.

Thomas, Margaret. "Crossing over to the Corporate Sector." *Library Journal* 126, no. 14 (2001): 46–50.

Tomaiuolo, Nicholas G. "Deconstructing Questia: The Usability of a Subscription Digital Library." *Searcher* 9, no. 7 (2001): 33–39.

Turner, Philip M. "Library and Information Studies: Education in the Age of Connectivity." Texas Library Association, March 25, 1997. Available at http://www.txla.org/pubs/tlj-4q96/turner.html (visited April 2002).

Wallace, Linda K. "Places an MLS Can Take You." *American Libraries* 33, no. 3 (2002): 40–45.

Wasserman, Paul. *The Librarian and the Machine: Observations of the Application of Machines in Administration of College and University Libraries.* Detroit: Gale Research, 1965.

Weissman, Sara. "Dear Vendor: Please Define Your Terms." *Library Journal Netconnect* (2000): 4–5.

Wengert, Robert G. "Some Ethical Aspects of Being an Information Professional." *Library Trends* 49, no. 3 (2001): 486–509.

Wilson, Thomas C. *The Systems Librarian: Defining Roles, Defining Skills.* Chicago: American Library Association, 1998.

INDEX

ANDREW K. PACE is the head of systems at the North Carolina State University Libraries (Raleigh, N.C.). After completing his M.S.L.S. degree at the Catholic University of America's School of Library and Information Science in 1996, Pace took a job with the library automation vendor Innovative Interfaces in Emeryville, California. There he started on the help desk and eventually moved up to become product integration specialist for several successful products, including WebPAC, KidsOnline, Advanced Keyword Search, Z39.50 Client and Server, and Electronic Course Reserves. In 1999 he left his private-sector job to return to a university setting at the NCSU Libraries. Pace has a regular column in *Computers in Libraries* magazine called "Coming Full Circle," and describes himself as both an iconoclastic traditionalist and a cynical optimist.